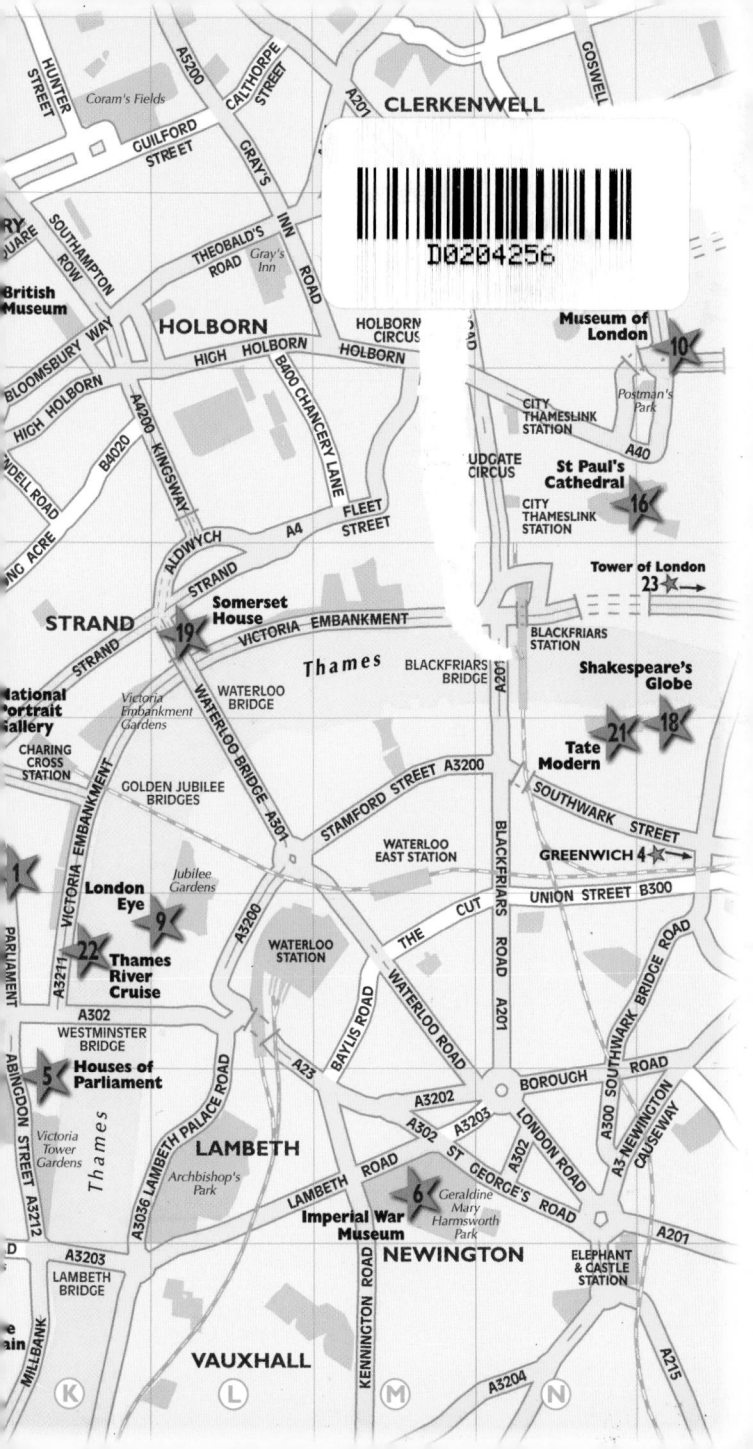
HUNTER STREET
A5200
CALTHORPE STREET
A201
CLERKENWELL
COSWELL
Coram's Fields
GUILFORD STREET
GRAY'S INN ROAD
SOUTHAMPTON ROW
THEOBALD'S ROAD
Gray's Inn
British Museum
HOLBORN
HOLBORN CIRCUS
HIGH HOLBORN
HOLBORN
BLOOMSBURY WAY
HIGH HOLBORN
B400 CHANCERY LANE
A4200 KINGSWAY
B4020
A4
FLEET STREET
ALDWYCH
STRAND
Museum of London
10
Postman's Park
CITY THAMESLINK STATION
A40
UDGATE CIRCUS
St Paul's Cathedral
16
CITY THAMESLINK STATION
Tower of London
23
STRAND
Somerset House
19
VICTORIA EMBANKMENT
Thames
BLACKFRIARS STATION
BLACKFRIARS BRIDGE
A201
Shakespeare's Globe
Victoria Embankment Gardens
WATERLOO BRIDGE
WATERLOO BRIDGE A301
21
18
Tate Modern
CHARING CROSS STATION
GOLDEN JUBILEE BRIDGES
STAMFORD STREET A3200
SOUTHWARK STREET
WATERLOO EAST STATION
GREENWICH 4
1
VICTORIA EMBANKMENT
London Eye
Jubilee Gardens
9
UNION STREET B300
THE CUT
BLACKFRIARS ROAD A201
A3200
22
Thames River Cruise
A3211
WATERLOO STATION
PARLIAMENT
A302
WESTMINSTER BRIDGE
BAYLIS ROAD
WATERLOO ROAD
A23
SOUTHWARK BRIDGE ROAD
5
Houses of Parliament
ABINGDON STREET A3212
A3036 LAMBETH PALACE ROAD
BOROUGH ROAD
A3202
A3203
A302
LONDON ROAD
A302
A300
A3 NEWINGTON CAUSEWAY
Victoria Tower Gardens
Thames
LAMBETH
Archbishop's Park
LAMBETH ROAD
ST GEORGE'S ROAD
6
Geraldine Mary Harmsworth Park
Imperial War Museum
A201
A3203
LAMBETH BRIDGE
NEWINGTON
ELEPHANT & CASTLE STATION
MILLBANK
KENNINGTON ROAD
VAUXHALL
A3204
A215
K
L
M
N

D0204256

Fodor's

25 Best

LONDON

INTRODUCING LONDON 4

An overview of the city and its history, as well as top tips on making the most of your stay.

TOP 25 12

We've pulled together all the Top 25 must-see sights and experiences in London.

MORE TO SEE 64

Even more options of great places to visit if you have plenty of time to spend in the city, whether it's in the city center or farther afield.

CITY TOURS 80

We've broken the city into areas with recommended tours in each one to help you get the best from your visit.

SHOP 118

Discover some of London's best shops and what they have to offer, from local produce to fashion and books.

KEY TO SYMBOLS

- Map reference to the accompanying pull-out map
- Address
- Telephone number
- Opening/closing times
- Restaurant or café
- Nearest subway (Metro) station
- Nearest bus route
- Nearest rail station

ENTERTAINMENT 128

Whether you're after a cultural fix or just want a place to relax with a drink after a hard day's sightseeing, we've made the best choices for you.

EAT 140

Uncover great dining experiences, from a quick bite at lunch to top-notch evening meals.

SLEEP 152

We've brought together the best hotels in the city, whatever budget you're on.

NEED TO KNOW 160

The practical information you need to make your trip run smoothly.

PULL-OUT MAP

The fold-out map accompanying this book is a comprehensive street plan of the city. We've given grid references within the book for each sight and listing.

- Nearest riverboat or ferry stop
- Facilities for visitors with disabilities
- Tourist information
- Other practical information
- Admission charges: Expensive (over £10), Moderate (£5–£10) and Inexpensive (under £5)
- ▷ Further information

Introducing London

Prepare for London to challenge your expectations. The dynamic British capital's traditions, from Savile Row outfitters to parading Horse Guards, thrive alongside a cutting-edge cultural calendar, arts venues, museums and world-class restaurants.

London buzzes with energy as whole areas of the capital have been revitalized. Spectacular modern architecture soars above ancient buildings. The cleaning of St. Paul's Cathedral revealed its true glory; Tate Modern provides great spaces in which to enjoy contemporary art; and the Millennium Footbridge, spanning the Thames between the two sights, gives a modern edge to one of the world's best panoramic city views. Along the river, trendy restaurants fill renovated warehouses, and gardens, museums, markets, theater and arts complexes have regenerated the South Bank.

In the redeveloped Docklands, the old Port of London is now a glittering world of skyscrapers, dominated by innovative Canary Wharf. Building for the 2012 Olympic Games has transformed districts in the East End and these are now some of the most vibrant places in the city to explore and discover (▷ 6–7).

Amid all this change, the greatness of London's 2,000 years of history has not been quashed. Visitors can still roam around one of Britain's finest medieval forts, the Tower of London, or visit a real royal home, Buckingham Palace. Equally, you can picnic in one of the royal parks or take a boat ride along the Thames to evoke times when this was the backbone of London and its great port.

Londoners themselves—while appreciating their good-value theater, free museums, great buildings and wealth of traditions—are likely to moan about just about everything else, from the high cost of property and living to the Congestion Charge and overcrowded public transport. Yet, in truth, they know they are living in one of the world's most vibrant cities. London, the political, financial and artistic capital of Britain, is hard to beat. Everything you could ever want is here; it is up to you to take it and enjoy it.

FACTS AND FIGURES

- Greater London covers 1,584sq km (611sq miles). With a population of over 8.46 million, it is Europe's largest city.
- London is the most culturally diverse city in Britain and more than 300 languages are spoken in the capital.
- London is the only city to have hosted the Summer Olympics three times (1908, 1948 and 2012).

CITY WITHIN A CITY

The City of London covers about 2.5sq km (1sq mile) and is Europe's largest central business and financial district. Referred to by Londoners either as "The City" or "The Square Mile," it has a daily working population that swells to over 300,000. The City has its own administration and police force and every year elects its own Lord Mayor.

DOWN UNDER

The London Underground (the Tube) is the oldest underground rail network in the world. The first line opened in 1863: 6km (4 miles) between Paddington and Farringdon Street on the Metropolitan Line. Today the Tube carries more than 1 billion passengers per year on 11 lines covering 402km (249 miles) of track and serving 270 stations.

BEATING THE COSTS

London is expensive. So, start by working out what is free. Top of the list are most major museums and galleries, the parks, monuments such as churches, and a variety of entertainment including lunch-time concerts and other events. To cut unavoidable costs, buy a Travel Pass and perhaps the London Sightseeing Pass (www.londonpass.com).

Look East

London's East End has shaken off its notoriety to become a hub of cutting-edge fashion, food, art and music. It's still gritty, but therein lies its attraction, and you will find plenty of places to tempt you to stop awhile, eat, browse and explore.

A Long History

East of the medieval walled City of London and north of the River Thames, the East End has long housed immigrant and refugee communities, from the Huguenot silk weavers who settled in Spitalfields in the late 17th century to the Bangladeshis who began arriving in the 1970s. Each wave of new arrivals added to the local culture and some buildings reflect the changing demographics: on Brick Lane, a chapel built by Huguenots in 1742 was first adapted for use by Methodists, then became the Spitalfields Great Synagogue and is now the Great London Mosque (Jamme Masjid).

Poverty and appalling living conditions attracted social reformers in the 19th century, leading to the formation of workers' associations and unions. As well as being a byword for urban deprivation, in the early 20th century the East End became known as a hotbed of radicalism, while its docks and industry made it a target for heavy bombing campaigns during the Second World War. Regeneration began in the 1990s with the development of Canary Wharf, a new Docklands business and financial district. Recently, East London has benefitted from London hosting the 2012 Olympic and Paralympic Games, with thousands of new homes being built in a green environment. The Queen Elizabeth Olympic Park hosts concerts and festivals and the sports facilities are superb.

Cutting-edge Cool

Once Whitechapel, Spitalfields, Hoxton and the area around Brick Lane in Shoreditch

Clockwise from top: Unusual housewares for sale on Columbia Road; enjoying the sunshine in the Allen Gardens; crowds of shoppers on Brick Lane, famous for

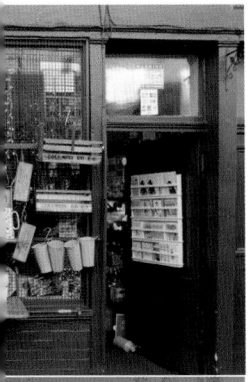

(nearest tube Aldgate East) were associated with slums and crime. Today a young, edgy and arty crowd have made these districts cool, with galleries and warehouse art exhibitions, cutting-edge fashion, trendy clubs and bars, an indie music scene, festivals, events and eye-popping street art.

In this foodie melting pot with cheap eats galore, try Korean fried chicken, steamed buns and *kimchi* in Shoreditch, Turkish grills in Dalston, Punjabi curry feasts and Vietnamese street food in Whitechapel, vegetarian and vegan fare in Walthamstow or the pie and mash and jellied eels that have been traditional East End staples since the 1800s.

Vibrant Markets

Head east on a Sunday and browse the vibrant markets—Columbia Road for plants and flowers, Petticoat Lane (▷ 126) for cheap clothes, ethnic fabrics and leatherwear and Spitalfields (▷ 126) where new meets vintage and innovative crafts sit alongside fusion food.

Brick Lane is famous for vintage fashion and alternative designers, second-hand furnishings, arts, crafts and kitsch collectibles. The Old Truman Brewery at 91 Brick Lane is a good place to start. Here you'll find the Sunday Upmarket featuring established designers and artists; Homegrown, a showcase for independent designers and makers; Backyard and Vintage Markets and the Boiler House Food Hall, where international specialties are displayed under high ceilings and the brewery's landmark chimney.

Lively street performers entertain the Brick Lane crowds and the ethnic eateries that line this long street span Jewish bagel and salt-beef shops and authentic Bangladeshi curry houses—of which there are so many that the area has become known as Banglatown and is often referred to as London's "curry hub."

its vintage fashion stores, kitsch collectibles and curry houses; the Aquatics Centre in the Queen Elizabeth Olympic Park; Petticoat Lane Market on Sunday

Top Tips For...

These great suggestions will help you tailor your ideal visit to London, no matter how you choose to spend your time. Each sight or listing has a fuller write-up elsewhere in the book.

Serious Retail Therapy
Start on the ground floor of **Harrods** (▷ 124) and work your way up.
Spend a whole day in **Harvey Nichols** (▷ 124) or **Selfridges** (▷ 126).
Search **Liberty** (▷ 126) for accessories.
Make a weekend foray into the five markets in **Camden Market** (▷ 124).
Tempt your tastebuds at **Borough Market's** (▷ 66) wonderful array of organic and artisan food stalls.

A Meal With a View
Book a table at the **Portrait Restaurant** atop the National Portrait Gallery (▷ 150).
Rendezvous at the café on level 6 of **Tate Modern** (▷ 151).
Go to Canary Wharf to eat at the waterside gastropub **The Gun** (▷ 147).
Take in the panoramic London views from atop the riverside Oxo Tower (▷ 149).
Eat stylishly amid trees and flamingos at rooftop **Babylon** (▷ 144).

A Breath of Fresh Air
Roam **Hampstead Heath** (▷ 77) and visit **Kenwood House** (▷ 77).
Climb high in **Greenwich Park** (▷ 20–21) to enjoy London views.
Enjoy botanical riches from around the world at **Kew Gardens** (▷ 77).
Go boating in **Regent's Park** (▷ 72) and visit the zoo.
Do the great central London royal park walk: through **St. James's** (▷ 42–43), **Green Park** (▷ 70) and **Hyde Park** (▷ 71), then **Kensington Gardens** (▷ 26–27).

Clockwise from top: Harrods—the ultimate department store; the Great Court of the British Museum; crowds gather to watch the Changing the Guard ceremony at

After Dark

Try **The Jazz Café** (▷ 135), **Jazz After Dark** (▷ 135) and **Pizza Express Club Soho** (▷ 137) for quality jazz.
Check out **Scala** (▷ 138) in the redeveloped area around King's Cross.
Dance the night away at **Guanabara** (▷ 135).
Barfly (▷ 133) in Camden showcases the indie scene with several acts nightly.
Head south of the river to the **Ministry of Sound** (▷ 136) for high-energy clubbing.

Watching the Bank Balance

Opt for bed-and-breakfast at **22 York Street** (▷ 155) or the no-frills chain **Premier Inn** (▷ 159).
Head to **Gaby's Deli** (▷ 147) on Charing Cross Road for hearty, no-nonsense food.
Go to a free concert in a church such as **St. James's, Piccadilly** (▷ 73).
Visit a free museum such as the **British Museum** (▷ 16–17).

Peeking Inside Londoners' Homes

Clarence House (▷ 68), to see where Prince Charles entertains.
Sir John Soane's two houses (▷ 74), filled with his antiquities.
Handel House (▷ 70), the famous composer's home for 26 years.
Buckingham Palace (▷ 18–19), the Queen's London home.
Apsley House (▷ 66), the perfect place to discover more about the Duke of Wellington.

Keeping the Kids Happy

Handle objects at the hands-on tables in the **British Museum** (▷ 16–17).
Climb the stairs to the top of **St. Paul's Cathedral** (▷ 44).
Go boating in **Regent's Park** (▷ 72).
Explore the hands-on exhibits at the Launch Pad in the **Science Museum** (▷ 47).

Buckingham Palace; the Making the Modern World gallery at the Science Musuem; time out in Green Park; the 19th-century Palm House at Kew Gardens

Timeline

1042 Edward the Confessor becomes king, making London the capital of England and Westminster his home; builds the abbey church of St. Peter.

1066 The Norman king, William the Conqueror, defeats King Harold at the Battle of Hastings; begins the Tower of London.

1485 Tudor rule commences, ending in 1603 with the death of Elizabeth I.

1533 Henry VIII breaks with Rome to marry Anne Boleyn; establishes the Church of England.

1649 Charles I is executed in Whitehall; the Commonwealth (1649–53) and Protectorate (1653–59) govern England until Charles II is restored to the throne in 1660.

1666 The Great Fire of London.

1759 The British Museum, London's first public museum, opens.

1851 The Great Exhibition is held in Hyde Park.

1863 World's first urban underground train service opens. In 1890 the first deep-dug train runs (known as "the Tube").

1939–45 Blitz bombings destroy

EARLY LONDON

- Emperor Claudius invades Britain in AD43; a deep-water port, Londinium, is soon established.
- In AD200 the Romans put a wall around Londinium, now capital of Britannia Superior; they withdraw in 410.

THE GREAT FIRE

The fire broke out at a baker's near Pudding Lane on the night of 2 September 1666. Raging for four days and nights, it destroyed four-fifths of the City of London and 13,200 homes. Sir Christopher Wren became the grand architect of the subsequent rebuilding of the city.

The London's Burning exhibit in the Museum of London shows the devastation caused by the fire

An attack by Luftwaffe bombers during the Blitz

a third of the City of London and much of the docks.

1951 Festival of Britain held on the site of the South Bank arts complex.

1960s The Beatles, Carnaby Street and the King's Road help create "swinging London."

1981 Regeneration and development of London Docklands begins.

1994 First Eurostar trains link London and Paris through the Channel Tunnel.

2000 Major millennium projects rejuvenate central London.

2002 Queen Elizabeth II celebrates her Golden Jubilee.

2007 Eurostar trains move to the refurbished St. Pancras station.

2011 Prince William marries Catherine Middleton at Westminster Abbey.

2012 The city hosts the Olympic Games and marks the Queen's Diamond Jubilee.

2013 Birth of HRH Prince George, third in line to the throne.

2014 Scotland votes to remain part of the UK.

2019 Expected completion of Crossrail, with around 100km (62 miles) of track linking 40 stations to transform London's transport system.

GROWING CITY

- During the 16th century, London was Europe's fastest-growing city; its population rose from 75,000 to 200,000.
- By 1750, London was Europe's biggest and wealthiest city, with about 700,000 people.
- London's population continued to grow, from around 1 million in 1800 to 6.5 million by 1900, peaking during World War II at 9 million.
- The city's population is currently over 8 million and rising.

The Great Exhibition of 1851

The new Eurostar terminal at St. Pancras station

TOP 25 Top 25

This section contains the must-see Top 25 sights and experiences in London. They are listed alphabetically, and numbered so you can locate them on the inside front cover.

1. Banqueting House	**14**
2. British Museum	**16**
3. Buckingham Palace	**18**
4. Greenwich	**20**
5. Houses of Parliament	**22**
6. Imperial War Museum	**24**
7. Kensington Palace and Gardens	**26**
8. Knightsbridge Shopping	**28**
9. London Eye	**30**
10. Museum of London	**32**
11. National Gallery	**34**
12. National Portrait Gallery	**36**
13. Natural History Museum	**38**
14. Portobello Road Market	**40**
15. St. James's Park	**42**
16. St. Paul's Cathedral	**44**
17. Science Museum	**46**
18. Shakespeare's Globe	**48**
19. Somerset House	**50**
20. Tate Britain	**52**
21. Tate Modern	**54**
22. Thames River Cruise	**56**
23. Tower of London	**58**
24. Victoria and Albert Museum	**60**
25. Westminster Abbey	**62**

1 Banqueting House

HIGHLIGHTS

- Rubens ceiling
- Allegory of James I between Peace and Plenty
- Allegory of the birth and coronation of Charles I
- Weathercock put on the roof by James II
- Vaulted undercroft, a drinking den for James I
- Whitehall river terrace in Embankment Gardens
- Video and self-guided audio tour

It is chilling to imagine Charles I calmly crossing the park from St. James's Palace to be beheaded outside the glorious hall built by his father. The magnificent ceiling was painted for Charles by Flemish artist Peter Paul Rubens.

Magnificent rooms This, all that remains of Whitehall Palace, was London's first building to be coated in smooth white Portland stone. Designed by Inigo Jones and built between 1619 and 1622, it marked the beginning of James I's dream to replace the original sprawling Tudor palace with a 2,000-room Palladian masterpiece. In fact, it was only the banqueting hall that was built. Inside, the King hosted small parties in the crypt and presided over lavish court ceremonies upstairs.

Clockwise from far left: The main hall, with ceiling paintings by Rubens; the elegant neoclassical exterior; a bust of Charles I, who was executed outside the Banqueting House in 1649; Rubens's nine allegorical ceiling paintings, which depict the unification of Scotland and England

Rubens ceiling The stunning ceiling was commissioned by James's son, Charles I. Painted between 1634 and 1636 by Peter Paul Rubens, the panels celebrate James I, who was also James VI of Scotland. Nine allegorical paintings show the unification of Scotland and England and the joyous benefits of wise rule. Rubens waited two years for his £3,000 fee.

The demise The palace has had a fair share of bad luck. Cardinal Thomas Wolsey lived so ostentatiously that he fell from Henry VIII's grace. Henry made it his, and his successors', main London royal home. Charles I was beheaded here on 30 January 1649, and William III suffered from the dank river air. A fire in 1698 wiped out the Tudor building, leaving only the Banqueting House.

THE BASICS

www.hrp.org.uk
K6
Whitehall, SW1
Mon–Sun 10–5; last admission 4.15. Closed 24 Dec–1 Jan, public hols and for functions and events
Westminster, Charing Cross, Embankment
None
Moderate
Occasional lunchtime and evening concerts

2 British Museum

HIGHLIGHTS

- Enlightenment Gallery
- Oriental antiquities
- African galleries
- Rosetta Stone
- Living and Dying Gallery
- Parthenon sculptures
- Assyrian and Egyptian rooms
- Norman Foster's Great Court redevelopment

TIPS

- Pick up a plan in the Great Court and choose just a few rooms to explore.
- Take an Eye Opener tour.
- Do the Hands-On object handling.
- Rent an audio guide.

The collection here is truly breathtaking, with a wealth of ancient treasures, among them bronzes from the Indian Chola dynasty and the lion-filled reliefs that once lined the walls of an Assyrian palace.

Physician founder Sir Hans Sloane, after whom Sloane Square is named, was a fashionable London physician, "interested in the whole of human knowledge" and an avid collector of everything from plants to prints. When he died in 1753 aged 92 he left his collection of more than 71,000 objects to the nation on condition that it was given a permanent home. Thus began the British Museum, opened in 1759 in a 17th-century mansion, Britain's first public museum and now its largest, covering 5.5ha (13.5 acres), with eight million objects.

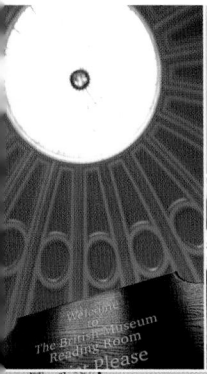

Clockwise from far left: The Queen Elizabeth II Great Court, designed by Foster + Partners as part of a redevelopment in the late 1990s; the historic circular Reading Room, at the heart of the Great Court; exhibits in the museum's Egyptian collection; the museum's imposing main entrance

Expansion George II, George III and George IV added to Sloane's collection, as did other monarchs. Their gifts, combined with the Townley and Parthenon sculptures, burst the building's seams, and so architect Robert Smirke designed a new museum, completed by his son, Sydney, in 1857. Even so, with booty from expeditions and excavations pouring in, the natural history collections moved to South Kensington (▷ 38–39). When the British Library (▷ 67) moved to St. Pancras in 1998, the Great Court was redeveloped and the King's Library transformed into a gallery on the Enlightenment.

Starting to explore Head to the glass-and steel-roofed Great Court, a magnificent space with an education center, lecture theaters, seminar rooms and cafés, to get your bearings.

THE BASICS

www.britishmuseum.org
J3
Great Russell Street, WC1 (another entrance in Montague Place)
020 7323 8299
Galleries: Sun–Thu 10–5.30, Fri 10–8.30. Great Court: Sun–Thu 9–6, Fri 9–8.30. Closed Good Friday, 24–26 Dec, 1 Jan
Restaurant, cafés
Holborn, Tottenham Court Road
Very good
Free, except for some temporary exhibitions
Full educational schedule

3 Buckingham Palace

TOP 25

HIGHLIGHTS

- The Queen's Gallery
- Changing the Guard
- State Coach, Royal Mews
- Nash's facade, Quadrangle
- Gobelin tapestries in the Guard Room
- Throne Room
- Van Dyck's portrait of Charles I and family

TIPS

- To avoid the lines, book a timed ticket in advance.
- Visit the quality royal souvenir shops.

Of the capital's houses now open to visitors, the Queen's London home is perhaps the most fascinating. Where else can you see a living sovereign's private art collection, drawing rooms and horse harnesses?

Yet another palace British sovereigns have had homes all over London over the years; moving from Westminster to Whitehall to Kensington and St. James's, and finally to Buckingham Palace. It was George III who bought the prime-site mansion, Buckingham House, in 1761 as a gift for his new bride, the 17-year-old Queen Charlotte, leaving St. James's Palace as the official royal residence.

Grand improvements King George IV and his architect John Nash made extravagant changes

Clockwise from far left: Buckingham Palace is the London home of the British sovereign—the red, gold and blue Royal Standard is raised when the Queen is in residence; visitors at the palace gates; the Grand Staircase, designed by John Nash; the Mall, the ceremonial route to the palace

using Bath stone, later covered up by Edward Blore's facade added for Queen Victoria. Today, the 600 rooms and 16ha (40-acre) garden include the State Apartments, offices for the royal household, a cinema, a swimming pool and the Queen's private rooms.

Open house The Queen inherited the world's finest private art collection. The Queen's Gallery, opened for her Golden Jubilee in 2002, exhibits some of her treasures. In the Royal Mews, John Nash's stables house gleaming fairy-tale coaches, harnesses and other apparel used for royal ceremonies. Don't miss the Buckingham Palace Summer Opening, when visitors can wander through the grand State Rooms resplendent with gold, pictures, porcelain, tapestries and thrones and enjoy the gardens.

THE BASICS

www.royal.gov.uk
www.royalcollection.org.uk
G7
Buckingham Gate, SW1
020 7766 7300; Ticket booking line 020 7766 7324
Queen's Gallery: daily 10–5.30, last admission 4.30. Royal Mews: 2 Feb–29 Mar Mon–Sat 10–4; 30 Mar–31 Oct daily 10–5, 1–30 Nov Mon–Sat 10–4; last admission 45 min before closing. Closed Dec–Jan and ceremonial occasions. State Rooms, Buckingham Palace: Aug daily 9.30–7.30, 1–27 Sep daily 9.30–6 (last admission 2 hours 15 min before closing)
Victoria, Hyde Park Corner, Green Park
Victoria
Excellent
Expensive
No photography

4 Greenwich

HIGHLIGHTS

- *Captain Augustus Keppel* by Sir Joshua Renolds (Queen's House)
- Maritime equipment at the National Maritime Museum
- The Painted Hall, where Nelson's body lay in state after the Battle of Trafalgar
- Winter stargazing at the Royal Observatory

A UNESCO World Heritage Site, this historic London district is a highly recommended day out, enthralling children and adults with science, sea stories and an excellent art collection. The town itself has a market, restaurants and a park.

Old Royal Naval College and the *Cutty Sark* Stop first at the *Cutty Sark*, once one of the fastest tea clippers in the world. Ravaged by fire in 2007, it took five years to restore. Continue into the main quadrangle of the Old Royal Naval College. With your back to the Thames, the remarkable Painted Hall, notable for its spectacular ceiling, is on the right.

Art and maritime heritage At the foot of Greenwich Park, the Queen's House and

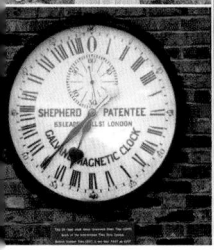

Clockwise from far left: The Royal Observatory, designed by Sir Christopher Wren; the Greenwich Meridian, the point chosen as 0° longitude; the Cutty Sark*'s figurehead; the Galvanic Magnetic Clock on the Greenwich Meridian, from which time around the world is measured*

National Maritime Museum stand adjacent to each other. The Queen's House is beautifully proportioned but the real surprise is the outstanding art collection inside. The National Maritime Museum is crammed with hands-on exhibits that answer pressing questions such as why the sea is salty. Boats on display range from small dinghies to the *Miss Britain III*, the first powerboat to top 100mph. Don't miss the fascinating collection of navigational equipment.

Astronomical delights Inside Sir Christopher Wren's cramped Observatory, small galleries explain how time is measured. But the new astronomy galleries of the Planetarium next door merit much more time; they're modern, engaging and exciting, without simplifying the bigger questions about the universe.

THE BASICS

www.visitgreenwich.org.uk
See page ▷ 115
Greenwich, SE10
Restaurants and cafés
DLR Greenwich, Cutty Sark
Greenwich, Maze Hill
From Westminster

Old Royal Naval College
www.ornc.org
020 8269 4799
Grounds daily 8–6; Painted Hall, Chapel and Discover Greenwich Visitor Centre daily 10–5; last admission 30 min before closing

The Queen's House, Royal Observatory, Planetarium, National Maritime Museum and *Cutty Sark*
www.rmg.co.uk
020 8858 4422
Daily 10–5; last admission 30 min before closing; Cutty Sark daily 10–5; Jul to mid-Sep 10–6. Last admission 1 hour before closing

5 Houses of Parliament

HIGHLIGHTS

- View from Westminster Bridge
- Big Ben
- Summer tours
- St. Stephen's Hall
- Westminster Hall
- State opening of Parliament
- Central Lobby
- Afternoon tea after a tour (advance booking essential)

Britain is governed from this landmark building alongside the River Thames. For many visitors, its clock tower and Big Ben chiming the hour symbolize London. Interesting tours reveal its architecture, traditions and the workings of government.

Powerhouse for crown and state William the Conqueror made Westminster his seat of rule to watch over the London merchants. It was soon the heart of government for England, then for Britain, then for a globe-encircling empire. It was also the principal home of the monarchs until Henry VIII moved to Whitehall. Here the foundations of Parliament were laid according to Edward I's Model Parliament of 1295: a combination of elected citizens, lords and clergy. This developed into the House of

Clockwise from top left: A nighttime view of the Houses of Parliament from the South Bank; Big Ben and the London Eye; Thomas Thornycroft's early 20th-century bronze of Boadicea by Westminster Bridge; Central Lobby, a meeting place between the House of Commons and the House of Lords

Commons (elected Members of Parliament) and the House of Lords (unelected senior members of State and Church). Henry VIII's Reformation Parliament of 1529–36 ended Church domination of Parliament and made the Commons more powerful than the Lords.

Fit for an empire Having survived the Catholic conspiracy to blow up Parliament on 5 November 1605, most of the buildings were destroyed by a fire in 1834. Kingdom and empire needed a new headquarters. With Charles Barry's plans and A.W. Pugin's detailed design, a masterpiece of Victorian Gothic was created. Behind the facade, the Lords is on the left and the Commons on the right. If Parliament is in session, there is a flag on Victoria Tower or, at night, a light on Big Ben.

THE BASICS

www.parliament.uk
K8
Westminster, SW1
020 7219 3000; Commons 020 7219 4272; Lords 020 7219 3107; tickets 020 7219 4114
Visits to House of Commons public gallery when house is sitting: Mon 2.30–10.30, Tue 11.30–7.30, Wed 11.30–7.30, Thu 9.30–5.30, Fri 9.30–3. Tours during summer recesses (usually Aug–Sep) and Sat throughout the year 9–4.15. Audio and guided tours in seven languages. UK citizens can arrange tours at other times through their MP
Westminster
Waterloo
Parliament free; tours expensive
Airport-style security screening in operation

6 Imperial War Museum

HIGHLIGHTS

- First World War galleries
- Atrium: Witnesses to War
- Turning Points 1934–1945: Key moments of the Second World War
- Family in Wartime exhibition
- Western Front trench
- The Holocaust Exhibition
- The Lord Ashcroft Gallery: Extraordinary Heroes
- Curiosities of War
- Modern conflicts: Kosovo, Iraq and Afghanistan

Covering conflicts and their impact from the First World War to the present day, this museum offers a thoughtful look at what life was like for soldiers and citizens, using personal objects, military might and testimonies from those who fought and those facing the challenges of life at home.

Extending its remit Originally conceived as a museum to collect and display material relating to the Great War, the Imperial War Museum opened to the public in the Crystal Palace in 1920. It moved to its present location, in what had been the Bethlem Royal Hospital (known as "Bedlam"), in 1936. By 1953 its remit had been extended to include all military operations in which Britain or the Commonwealth have been involved since 1914.

Clockwise from left: The impressive entrance and grounds of the Imperial War Museum; admiring the naval guns outside the museum; detail on an "Ole Bill" bus from World War I; tanks on display in the large exhibits gallery

New galleries A £40-million refurbishment saw the opening in July 2014 of the new, much-enlarged First World War galleries, together with a redesign of the dramatic, four-story-high atrium, created by the innovative architecture and design team at Foster + Partners. The displays include a Spitfire, Harrier Jump Jet and V-1 "doodlebug" and V-2 bombs suspended above field guns, and a T34 tank.

Created to coincide with the centenary of the First World War, the galleries feature more than 1,300 original objects, including letters and diaries from the frontline, interactive multimedia displays that give insight into life both in the trenches and at home, and help visitors understand the war and its global impact. Among the objects on display are weapons, uniforms, keepsakes and trinkets, photographs and art.

THE BASICS

www.iwm.org.uk
M8
Lambeth Road, SE1
020 7416 5000
Daily 10–6, last admission 5.30. Closed 24, 25, 26 December
Café, Tea Room in summer
Lambeth North, Waterloo
Waterloo, Elephant and Castle
Excellent
Free; charge for some temporary exhibitions
Full education schedules, talks and events

7 Kensington Palace and Gardens

TOP 25

HIGHLIGHTS

- The King's grand staircase
- The Queen's sate apartments
- Wind dial, King's Gallery
- Luminous Lace light piece
- Princess Victoria's dolls' house
- Royal dresses
- Tea in the Orangery
- The Sunken Garden

It's difficult not to be charmed by this royal residence with its grand state apartments, galleries and sunken garden—truly a fitting home for a throughly modern king.

Perfect location The year William III became king in 1689, he and his wife Mary bought a mansion in this tiny Kensington village. William suffered with asthma, so the cleaner air here suited him, while the couple also wanted to be perfectly positioned for London socializing and country living. Sir Christopher Wren and Nicholas Hawksmoor were brought in to remodel and enlarge the house. Despite the small rooms, George I introduced palatial grandeur with Colen Campbell's staircase and state rooms. Queen Anne added the Orangery (the architect was Nicholas Hawksmoor, and

Clockwise from far left: A view of the palace from Dial Walk in Kensington Gardens; a statue commemorating William III, the palace's first royal resident; George Frampton's famed statue of Peter Pan in Kensington Gardens; the Orangery; the peaceful Italian Garden, a Victorian addition

the woodcarver was Grinling Gibbons) and annexed a chunk of royal Hyde Park, a trick repeated by George II's wife, Queen Caroline, who created the Round Pond and Long Water to complete the 110ha (275-acre) Kensington Gardens. Today, trees are the backdrop for sculptures (such as George Frampton's fairy-tale *Peter Pan,* ▷ 72), monuments, and contemporary exhibitions at the lakeside Serpentine Gallery and Serpentine Sackler Gallery.

New look A £12-million project has opened up previously unseen areas of the palace, including fine state apartments and landscaped public gardens. The routes focus on different historical eras and figures, including Diana, Princess of Wales, and Queen Victoria, whose story is told in her own words.

THE BASICS

www.hrp.org.uk
www.serpentinegalleries.org
A6
Kensington Gardens, W8
Serpentine Gallery 020 7402 6075
Daily Mar–Oct 10–6, Nov–Feb 10–5; closed 24–26 Dec, 26–30 Jan; Serpentine Galleries during exhibitions Tue–Sun 10–6
Café, Orangery (▷ 149)
High Street Kensington, Queensway
Good
Expensive; family tickets. Serpentine free
Personalized tours by expert Explainers

8 Knightsbridge Shopping

HIGHLIGHTS

- Food halls at Harrods
- Designer dresses at Harvey Nichols
- Boutiques on Walton Street

TIPS

- In Harrods, check out the day's events, shows and demos.
- If you need a special outfit, no staff are more helpful than at Harvey Nichols.
- If it rains, stay put in Harrods and visit the spa.

Knightsbridge is London's smartest and most expensive neighborhood, with real estate, shops and price tags to match. It's the place for some serious retail therapy.

Stylish shops As you leave the Underground station (Sloane Street exit) you'll see Harvey Nichols (▷ 124), London's most fashionable department store. On emerging from Harvey Nichols, head back towards the Underground and continue along Brompton Road. Opposite is a huge Burberry store, known for its tan-and-gray check designs. On the left, as you walk towards the canopied shopfront of Harrods (▷ 124), is Swarovski, with its window displays of crystal jewelry. Leave Harrods by the Hans Road exit and you'll see luxury lingerie and swimwear store Rigby & Peller across the street.

Clockwise from far left: Harvey Nichols's flagship Knightsbridge store; Swarovski jewelry shop on Brompton Road; the landmark art nouveau Michelin building, now home to the popular Bibendum restaurant; Harrods; the Fifth Floor Bar at Harvey Nichols

Even more stylish shops Return to Brompton Road and pass leather store Mulberry, before turning left into Beauchamp Place for smart restaurants, designer fashion and the Map House, with its precious maps and engravings. At the end of Beauchamp Place, turn right into attractive Walton Street, lined with interior design, jewelry and children's clothes shops. With Chanel to your right across Brompton Road, turn left into Sloane Avenue by the iconic Michelin building famed for its design, décor and Bibendum restaurant (▷ 145). The flagship Conran Shop, selling contemporary design for the home, is on the right, with fashion from Joseph for Men on the left. Continue down Sloane Avenue to reach the King's Road or turn left for Sloane Square, home to Peter Jones, the department store (▷ 126).

THE BASICS

- D7–9
- Knightsbridge
- Harvey Nichols' 5th floor is dedicated to food. Go to Harrods for elegant dining and macaroons. The Berkeley Hotel, Wilton Place, tel 020 7235 6000, serves Pret-à-Portea, a fashionista afternoon tea (daily 1–5)
- Knightsbridge

9 London Eye

TOP 25

HIGHLIGHTS

- Panoramic views across the city in every direction
- On a clear day you can see for 40km (25 miles)
- Spotting landmarks along the Thames
- Aerial view of the Palace of Westminster

TIPS

- It is best to book ahead, although not essential.
- Evening riders enjoy the London lights.
- Tickets include access to the 4-D Experience, a 3-D film with special effects.

Attracting 3.75 million visitors a year, London's most visible attraction, soaring 135m (443ft) above the South Bank of the Thames, affords spectacular city views.

Riding high Passengers ride in one of the 32 capsules that rotate smoothly through 360 degrees in a slow-moving 30-minute flight. Each capsule is fully enclosed and comfortably holds 25 people. Because the capsules are secured on the outside of the wheel (rather than hung from it like a Ferris Wheel), views through the large glass windows are totally unobstructed. Passengers can walk freely inside the capsules, which are kept level by a motorized motion stability system—although seating is provided. Each capsule is in touch with the ground via camera and radio links. The wheel is

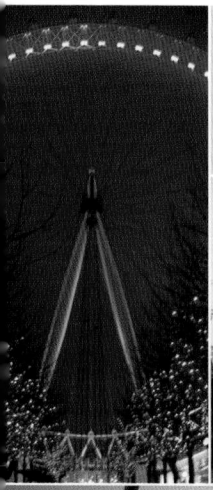

Clockwise from far left: Opened in 2000, the Eye quickly became an established part of the South Bank's landscape; the Eye at night; the glass capsules, attached to the outside of the wheel, offer unobstructed views; an aerial view of the Palace of Westminster at dusk

in constant motion, revolving continuously at 0.26m (0.85ft) per second, a quarter of the average walking speed, enabling passengers to walk straight on and off the moving capsules. After dark, the trees lining the approach to the London Eye are bathed in magical blue lights, while the boarding platform appears to float on a cloud of more blue light.

Revolutionary design Conceived by David Marks and Julia Barfield to celebrate the millennium, the Eye represents the turning of the century and is a universal and ancient symbol of regeneration. It took seven years and the expertise of people from five European countries for their design to be realized. The Eye is on the riverside Thames Path, which continues east all the way to the Thames Barrier.

THE BASICS

www.londoneye.com
L7
Riverside Gardens, next to County Hall, SE1
Apr–Jun daily 10–9 (Fri–Sat 9.30); Jul–Aug 10–9.30 (Fri in Aug to 11.30pm); Sep–Mar 10–8.30
Riverfront cafés
Waterloo, Westminster, Embankment, Charing Cross
Waterloo
Very good. Boarding ramp available for wheelchair users
Expensive

10 Museum of London

TOP 25

HIGHLIGHTS

- London Before London Gallery
- Hoard of 43 gold Roman coins
- Spitalfields Woman (Roman)
- Viking grave
- The lavish, late-18th-century Fanshawe dress
- Model of Tudor London
- Pleasure Gardens
- The London 2012 Olympics Cauldron gallery

A visit here is easily the best way to cruise through London's 2,000 years of history, pausing to see a Roman shoe or the Lord Mayor's State Coach, or to peek through a Victorian shop window; and it is even built on the West Gate of London's Roman fort.

A museum for London This is the world's largest and most comprehensive city museum, opened in 1976 in a building by Powell and Moya. The collection combines the old Guildhall Museum's City antiquities with the London Museum's costumes and other culturally related objects. The continuous building work and redevelopment in the City since the 1980s, allied with increased awareness about conservation, has ensured a steady flow of archaeological finds into the collection.

Clockwise from left: The lavish 18th-century Lord Mayor's State Coach on display at the museum; a window to the city's past—the original museum building, built in the 1970s; coins from the first century AD, part of the impressive Roman exhibit

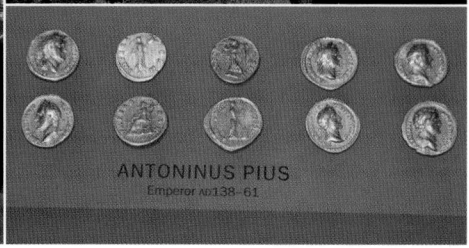

A museum about London The building is, appropriately, in the barbican of the Roman fort, and the rooms are laid out chronologically to keep the story clear. The London Before London gallery follows the story of prehistoric Londoners before Roman settlement. One of the most impressive galleries is Roman London, which explains the founding of Londinium in about AD50 until AD410 when the Roman army quit Britain. The Expanding City chronicles the Great Fire of 1666 to the 1850s, an era of wealth, power and global influence. People make a city, so in every room it is Londoners who are really telling the story, whether it is through Roman ceramics or Tudor clothes. A major redevelopment has resulted in superb displays and a mesmerizing re-creation of the 18th-century Vauxhall Pleasure Gardens.

THE BASICS

www.museumoflondon.org.uk
P3
150 London Wall, EC2
020 7001 9844
Daily 10–6; galleries begin to close at 5.40. Closed 24–26 Dec
2 cafés
Barbican, St. Paul's
Liverpool Street, City Thameslink, Farringdon
Excellent
Free
Full education schedule; audio tour

11 National Gallery

TOP 25

HIGHLIGHTS

- *Virgin Enthroned*, Cenni di Peppi Cimabue
- Cartoon, Leonardo da Vinci
- *Pope Julius II*, Raphael
- *The Arnolfini Wedding*, Van Eyck
- Equestrian portrait of Charles I by Van Dyck
- *The Haywain*, John Constable
- *Madonna of the Pinks*, Raphael
- *The Archers*, Henry Raeburn
- *Sunflowers*, Van Gogh
- *Mr and Mrs William Hallett*, Gainsborough
- *La Pointe de Hève*, Monet
- Restored entrance lobby and galleries

Here is a collection of very fine pictures—and for free, so you can drop in for a few minutes' peace in front of Leonardo da Vinci's cartoon in the Sainsbury Wing or Rubens's ravishing *Samson and Delilah*.

Quality collection Founded in 1824 with just 38 pictures, the National Gallery now has over 2,300 paintings, all on show. Spread throughout William Wilkins's neoclassical building and the Sainsbury Wing extension, they provide an extremely high quality, concise panorama of European painting from Giotto to Cézanne.

Free from the start Unusual for a national painting collection, the nucleus is not royal but the collection of John Julius Angerstein, a self-made financier. From the start it was open to

Clockwise from far left: The gallery's impressive neoclassical facade, fronting Trafalgar Square; one of the elegant galleries in the East Wing; the East Wing of the National Gallery; a detail of Vincent van Gogh's 1888 painting Sunflowers; *the exterior of the museum*

all, free of charge, and provided a wide spectrum of British painting within a European context—aims that are still maintained today. However, there may be a charge for the temporary exhibitions in the Sainsbury Wing.

A first visit To take advantage of the rich artistic panorama, choose a room from each of the four chronologically arranged sections. Early paintings by Duccio di Buoninsegna, Jan van Eyck, Piero della Francesca and others fill the Sainsbury Wing. The West Wing has 16th-century pictures, including Michelangelo's *Entombment*, while the North Wing is devoted to 17th-century artists such as Van Dyck, Rubens, Rembrandt and painters of the Dutch school. The East Wing runs from Chardin through Gainsborough to Matisse and Picasso.

THE BASICS

www.nationalgallery.org.uk
J6
Trafalgar Square, WC2
020 7747 2885
Sat–Thu 10–6, Fri 10–9. Closed 24–26 Dec, 1 Jan
Restaurant, café
Charing Cross, Leicester Square
Charing Cross
Excellent
Free
Guided tours (free daily 11.30 and 2.30, also Fri 7pm, Sat–Sun 4pm), lectures, films, audio guide, interactive screens. Free 10-minute talks (days vary 1pm), free lunchtime talks (Tue–Sat 1pm)

12 National Portrait Gallery

TOP 25

HIGHLIGHTS

- *Self-portrait with Barbara Hepworth*, Ben Nicholson
- Richard II
- The Tudor Galleries
- *Queen Victoria*, Sir George Hayter
- *The Brontë Sisters*, by their brother, Branwell Brontë
- *Isambard Kingdom Brunel*, John Callcott
- *Sir Peter Hall*, Tom Phillips
- Using the self-guiding audio tour
- An unfinished sketch of Jane Austen (*c.*1810) by her sister, Cassandra

It's fascinating to see what someone famous looked like and how they chose to be painted—for instance, you would never expect Francis Drake to be dressed in red courtier's, rather than nautical, clothes.

British record Founded in 1856 to collect portraits of the great and good in British life, and so inspire others to greatness, this is now the most comprehensive collection of its kind in the world, comprising watercolors, oil paintings, caricatures, silhouettes and photographs.

Start at the top The galleries, incorporating the Ondaatje Wing, are arranged chronologically, starting on the second floor—reached by stairs or elevator. Tudor monarchs kick off a visual *Who's Who* of British history that moves

Clockwise from far left: The main entrance to the National Portrait Gallery; the Tudor Galleries; portraits and busts from the Regency period on display in the acclaimed Weldon Galleries; an 1834 portrait of the Brontë sisters by their brother, Branwell; a mosaic at the museum entrance

through inventors, merchants, explorers and empire builders to modern politicians. Here you'll find Isambard K. Brunel, Robert Clive and Warren Hastings of India, Winston Churchill and Margaret Thatcher. There is Chaucer in his floppy hat, Kipling at his desk and A.A. Milne with his engaging tales Christopher Robin and Winnie-the-Pooh on his knee. Lesser-known sitters also merit a close look, such as the 18th-century portrait of the extensive Sharp Family, who formed an orchestra and played at Fulham every Sunday.

Modern times Among the many famous portraits from history, you may also spot a number of more familiar, contemporary faces, such as the footballer David Beckham and one of the former Beatles, Sir Paul McCartney.

THE BASICS

www.npg.org.uk
J5
St. Martin's Place, WC2
020 7306 0055
Sat–Wed 10–6, Thu–Fri 10–9. Closed 24–26 Dec
Café, rooftop restaurant
Leicester Square, Charing Cross
Charing Cross
Good
Free except for special exhibitions
Lectures, events, explorer touchscreens

13 Natural History Museum

HIGHLIGHTS

- Giant Earth sculpture
- Dinosaur skeletons
- Fossilized frogs
- The Vault, a gallery of crystals, gems and meteorites
- Restless Surface Gallery
- Tank Room in the Darwin Centre

TIPS

- Use the side entrance on Exhibition Road.
- The museum is huge: Plan your visit carefully.

The museum building looks like a Romanesque cathedral and is wittily decorated with a zoo of animals to match its contents—extant animals on the west side, extinct ones on the east side.

Two museums in one Overflowing the British Museum, the Life Galleries were moved here in 1881. They tell the story of life on earth. The story of the Earth itself is told in the Earth Galleries, beginning with a 300-million-year-old fossil of a fern. The Darwin Centre uses IT to make the most of the museum's 70 million objects and make the work of its 300 or so scientists accessible worldwide. Take the glass lift to its futuristic Cocoon building, then wend your way down its sloping walkways, taking in the exciting insect and plant displays.

Clockwise from far left: The Hinze Hall, the museum's cavernous entrance hall; the escalator leading to the Red Zone, where galleries explore the nature of the Earth; insect specimens on display at Cocoon, part of the Darwin Centre; the original 1880 Waterhouse Building

Follow the zone Color-coded zones help you plan your visit. In the Red Zone, dramatic sculptures and a giant metallic globe lead to galleries revealing how the planet has evolved: a treasury of minerals, gems and rocks; displays on how volcanoes and earthquakes happen; and the effect of man on nature. Exhibits in the Green Zone go from dinosaurs to birds and insects via fossils and our human ancestors. The Blue Zone celebrates the amazing diversity of our planet as it explores fish, amphibians and reptiles; investigates human biology; and gets up close to the blue whale, the largest creature on Earth. Don't miss the Images of Nature gallery, at the end of the Blue Zone, which houses a stunning collection of art inspired by nature. The superb Darwin Centre and quiet wildlife garden occupy the Orange Zone.

THE BASICS

www.nhm.ac.uk
B8
Cromwell Road, SW7; also entrance on Exhibition Road
020 7942 5000
Daily 10–5.50. Closed 24–26 Dec
Meals, snacks, deli café, picnic areas
South Kensington
Excellent
Free; charge for some temporary exhibitions
Regular tours, lectures, films, workshops

14 Portobello Road Market

TOP 25

HIGHLIGHTS

- Red Lion Antiques Arcade, where it all began
- Spooky stuffed animals sold in Natural History
- The clocks and watches in Admiral Vernon Arcade
- Arts and crafts and art deco in the Crown Arcade

TIPS

- Saturday is by far the best day, when the antiques dealers set up stalls in the street.
- No price is totally fixed; bargain hard.
- It is true that the early bird finds the best prices.
- Join locals buying a treat at New Tom's Café on Westbourne Grove.

Spend a Saturday wandering down Portobello Road, peering at the stalls and dipping into the shops behind them to seek out a special piece of china, a fascinating piece of glass or a pretty piece of jewelry.

Portobello Road Originally a lane leading down to Porto Bella Farm, this road has been a market site for over a century. Gypsies traded horses and herbs here in the 1870s, but the antiques dealers only arrived in the late 1940s. Today, Portobello Road Market claims to be the world's largest antiques market. It is really a series of markets that spill into surrounding streets where almost everything imaginable is sold. If you want a day-long party of fascination, fun and friendliness, come and take in the atmosphere.

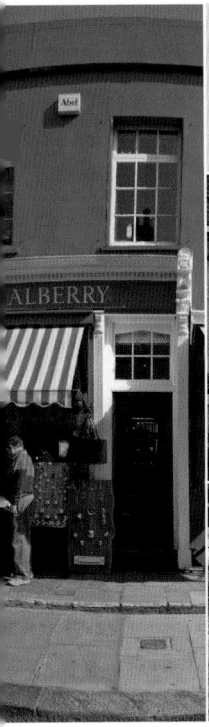

Clockwise from left: Antiques arcades and galleries line Portobello Road; the Saturday-morning antiques market, when antiques traders and bargain-hunters crowd the area, sees Portobello Road at its busiest; fruit and vegetables are sold in the market's lower reaches

More than just stalls Starting at the top, there are the established specialist antiques shops for maps, silver, medals and collectables, where bargains are few. Don't miss Lipka Arcade and the 20th Century Theatre, opposite. Farther down, where the stalls begin, the stock is more varied and you can join locals in the pubs and cafés to discuss values and possible purchases. Here you'll find antique clothes, records and china next to contemporary ceramics and jewellery. Explore the by-roads, too.

For something different After the vegetable and organic food stalls you go under the Westway flyover and find restorative cafés. The tone changes. Here, look for funky bric-a-brac, cutting-edge street fashion, vintage clothes and even secondhand bicycles.

THE BASICS

www.portobelloroad.co.uk; shopportobello.co.uk

See page ▷ 114

Market office: 72 Tavistock Road, W11

020 7727 7684

Mon–Wed 9–6, Thu 9–1, Fri–Sat 9–7. Closed bank hols

Notting Hill Gate, Ladbroke Grove

15 St. James's Park

TOP 25

HIGHLIGHTS

- Springtime daffodils
- Whitehall views from the lake bridge
- Feeding the pelicans, daily 2.30–3
- Views to Buckingham Palace
- Exotic plants in the tropical border

TIPS

- Inn the Park café opens early and closes late.
- It's the perfect setting for summer picnics.
- Cyclists are welcome in the royal parks.

Drop in to St. James's Park to picnic and laze on a deckchair, try spotting palaces across the duck-filled lake or following part of the Diana, Princess of Wales Memorial Walk.

Royal heart St. James's Park is the oldest and most royal of London's nine royal parks, surrounded by the Palace of Westminster, St. James's Palace, Buckingham Palace and the remains of Whitehall Palace. Kings and their courtiers have been frolicking here since 1536, when Henry VIII laid out a deer park in what was then marshy water meadow and built a hunting lodge that became St. James's Palace. In the early 17th century, James I began the menagerie, including crocodiles and an elephant who drank a gallon of wine daily.

Left to right: With Buckingham Palace at its western end and the Houses of Parliament within easy reach, the park is a popular retreat for visitors; a drinking fountain; springtime, when the daffodils are in bloom, is one of the best times to visit

French order In the mid-17th century, Charles II, influenced by Versailles, near Paris, redesigned the park to include a canal, Birdcage Walk (where he kept aviaries) and the graveled Mall, where he played pell mell, a game similar to croquet. George IV, helped by John Nash and influenced by Humphrey Repton, softened the formal French lines into the English style in the 19th century, making this 37ha (93-acre) park of blossoming shrubs and curving paths popular with romantics.

Nature As the park is an important migration point and breeding area for birds, two full-time ornithologists look after up to 1,000 birds from more than 45 species. Pelicans live on Duck Island, a tradition begun when the Russian Ambassador gave some to Charles II in 1664.

THE BASICS

www.royalparks.org.uk
J7
The Mall, SW1
0300 061 2350
Daily 5am–midnight
Inn the Park (▷ 148)
St. James's Park, Green Park, Westminster
Victoria
Very good
Free
Changing the Guard (on Horseguards Parade). Bird talks and guided walks

16 St. Paul's Cathedral

HIGHLIGHTS

- Sung evensong
- Frescoes and mosaics
- Wren's Great Model in the Triforium (upstairs)
- Triple-layered dome weighing 76,000 tons
- Jean Tijou's wrought-iron sanctuary gates
- Wellington's memorial
- *Light of the World*, Holman Hunt
- The view across London
- Wren's epitaph under the dome

To slip into St. Paul's for evensong, and sit gazing up at the mosaics as the choir's voices soar, is to enjoy a moment of absolute peace and beauty. Go early or late to avoid the crowds.

Wren's London After the restoration of the monarchy in 1660, artistic patronage bloomed under Charles II. Following the Great Fire of London in 1666, which destroyed four-fifths of the City, Christopher Wren took main stage as King's Surveyor-General. The spires and steeples of his 51 churches, of which 23 still stand, surrounded his masterpiece, St. Paul's.

The fourth St. Paul's This cathedral church for the diocese of London was founded in AD604 by King Ethelbert of Kent. The first three

Clockwise from far left: The view of St. Paul's Cathedral from Festival Gardens; the interior of the magnificent dome, decorated with frescoes by Sir James Thornhill; the choir stalls and high altar; St. Paul's before the Fire of London in 1666; architect Sir Christopher Wren

churches burned down. Wren's, built in stone and paid for with a special coal tax, was the first English cathedral built by a single architect, the only one with a dome, and the only one in the English baroque style. A £40-million cleaning-and-repair project marked the cathedral's 300th anniversary in 2010. Statues and memorials of Britain's famous crowd the interior and crypt—heroes Wellington and Nelson, artists Turner and Reynolds, as well as Wren himself.

The climb The 528 steps to the Golden Gallery at the top are worth the effort. Shallow steps rise to the Whispering Gallery for views of Sir James Thornhill's dome, decorated with frescoes and 19th-century mosaics. For virtual access to the dome, visit Oculus, a 270-degree film experience in the crypt.

THE BASICS

www.stpauls.co.uk
N4
Ludgate Hill, EC4
020 7246 8350
Mon–Sat 8.30–4 (last entry). Galleries and Oculus: 9.30–4.15. Services include Mon–Sat 7.30, 8, 12.30, 5, Sun 8, 10.15, 11.30, 3.15, 6
Restaurant, café
St. Paul's
City Thameslink
Very good
Expensive
Multimedia, audio and guided tours included; organ recitals

17 Science Museum

HIGHLIGHTS

- Demonstrations
- Launch Pad's interactive exhibits and shows
- The glass bridge in the Challenge of Materials
- Pattern Pod, the hands-on gallery for children aged 5–8
- Atmosphere Gallery
- Puffing Billy
- 18th-century watches and clocks

TIP

- Head for the higher, quieter floors to escape the crowds.

Even if you are no scientist, it's thrilling to understand how a plane flies, how Newton's reflecting telescope worked or how we receive satellite television. You'll find the answers using interactive exhibits. This is science at its most accessible.

Industry and science Opened in 1857, this museum comes closest to fulfilling Prince Albert's educational aims when he founded the South Kensington Museums after the Great Exhibition of 1851. Its full title is the National Museum of Science and Industry. Over the seven floors, which contain more than 60 collections, the story of human industry, discovery and invention is recounted through various tools and products, from exquisite Georgian cabinets to a satellite launcher.

Clockwise from far left: Landmark designs are displayed in the Making the Modern World Gallery; displays in the Who Am I? Gallery explore the wonders of human genetics and intelligence; one of the child-friendly exhibits in the Launchpad; an early 20th-century engine in the Energy Hall

Science made fun See how vital everyday objects were invented and then developed for use in Making the Modern World; find out what makes you smarter than a chimp in Who Am I?; and get involved in the very latest scientific hot topics in Antenna. The galleries vary from rooms of beautiful 18th-century objects to an astronaut's moon capsule and in-depth explanations of abstract concepts. You can even learn the basic principles of flying by testing out the hands-on equipment in the Flight Gallery. Health Matters reveals how technology has dramatically changed medicine. The interactive Challenge of Materials and the high-tech Launch Pad, a favorite with children, explore science, technology and the complex world, while the Atmosphere gallery tackles climate science brilliantly.

THE BASICS

www.sciencemuseum.org.uk
C8
Exhibition Road, SW7
Daily 10–6
Restaurants, cafés, picnic area in basement
South Kensington
Excellent (tel helpline 020 7942 4000)
Free; IMAX cinema expensive
Guided tours, demonstrations, historic characters, lectures, films, workshops

18 Shakespeare's Globe

HIGHLIGHTS

- Guided tour storytellers
- Attending a performance
- Interactive displays
- Costume collection

TIP

- Tours and performances take place in all weathers, so dress appropriately.

A faithful reconstruction of The Bard's open-air theater, where Shakespeare's plays are performed and cutting-edge new writers have the opportunity to shine.

One man's vision From his first visit to London in 1949, actor and director Sam Wanamaker dreamed of re-creating Shakespeare's 16th-century Globe theater as close as possible to its original site by the Thames at Bankside. Several decades and a long struggle later, the theater opened in 1997 with a production of *Henry V*.

Tradition to the core Constructed of English oak with mortise-and-tenon joints, lime plaster and water reed thatch roof (the first permitted since the Great Fire of London in 1666), the building techniques used were painstakingly

Left: Watching a play at Shakespeare's Globe gives you a unique insight into Elizabethan theater; below: The Globe has been reconstructed on London's Bankside, a short distance from the site of the original building that hosted Shakespeare's plays

accurate. Its thrust stage projects into a large circular yard surrounded by three tiers of simple benches (cushions can be hired) for 857 people. Only the seating area and stage are covered, so the 700 "groundlings" standing in the yard below the stage swelter in the heat and get very wet when it rains. An exhibition beneath the theater tells its history and explores the London Shakespeare would have known.

New theater A £7.5-million indoor Jacobean theater, the Sam Wanamaker Playhouse, has created an intimate, year-round theatrical experience, quite different from that of the Globe. Performing the plays of Shakespeare and his contemporaries in the surroundings for which they were originally intended, it seats 340 people and is predominantly lit by candles.

THE BASICS

www.shakespearesglobe.com
P6
21 New Globe Walk, SE1
Exhibition and tour office 020 7902 1500
Theatre Box Office 020 7401 9919
Exhibition daily 9–5.30; tours daily 9.30–5, every 30 minutes. Main stage performance season mid-Apr to mid-Oct
Restaurant, bar, café
Blackfriars, Mansion House, London Bridge, Southwark
London Bridge
Bankside Pier
Good. Access information line tel 020 7902 1409
Expensive (includes guided theater tour and exhibition audio guide)
Temporary exhibitions, full educational schedule

19 Somerset House

HIGHLIGHTS

- The Courtauld Collection
- The Fridart Collection
- *A Bar at the Folies-Bergère*, Manet
- Rubens paintings
- *The Trinity*, Botticelli

Somerset House was transformed from a lavish but forgotten building into a riverside palace. Spend some time here and enjoy French Impressionist masterpieces, summer concerts and dancing fountains.

Palatial home A majestic triple-arch gateway leads from the Strand into Sir William Chambers' English Palladian government offices (1776–86). The Courtauld Collection is housed in rooms lavishly decorated for the Royal Academy, before its move to Piccadilly. Ahead, the great courtyard has fountains, a theater, an ice-rink and café tables, according to the season. A superb fine dining restaurant on the summer terrace, with sweeping Thames views, is a seasonal treat. Changing exhibitions are held in the Embankment Galleries.

Clockwise from far left: The courtyard of Somerset House; artistic treasures on display in the Courtauld Gallery; the Courtauld's lavishly decorated rooms, which were originally used by the Royal Academy; the elegant staircase leading to the upper floors of the Courtauld Gallery

Courtauld Gallery Industrialist Samuel Courtauld's collection of French Impressionist and post-Impressionist paintings, with works by Renoir, Cézanne, Van Gogh, Manet, Seurat and Gauguin, are on display. There are also 18th-century portraits by Goya and Gainsborough, canvases and sketches by Rubens, works by Botticelli and Tintoretto and an important Gothic and medieval collection. Twentieth-century highlights include works by Matisse, Dufy, Kandinsky and the Bloomsbury group.

Drawings, prints and sculpture The excellent collection of prints includes works by Michelangelo, Dürer and Leonardo da Vinci, while the sculpture collection spans antiquity to the 20th century. The decorative arts are represented by fine Islamic ceramics and metalwork.

THE BASICS

www.somersethouse.org.uk
L5
Somerset House, Strand, WC2
020 7845 4600
Daily 10–6; extended hours for Courtyard, River Terrace and restaurant
Cafés, restaurants
Temple
Blackfriars, Charing Cross, Waterloo
Excellent
Somerset House free; Courtauld Gallery moderate
Free guided tours of Somerset House Tue 12.45, 2.15, Thu 1.15, 2.45, Sat 12.15, 1.15, 2.15 and 3.15. Tickets available from 10.30am from the information desk in the Seaman's Hall, South Building

20 Tate Britain

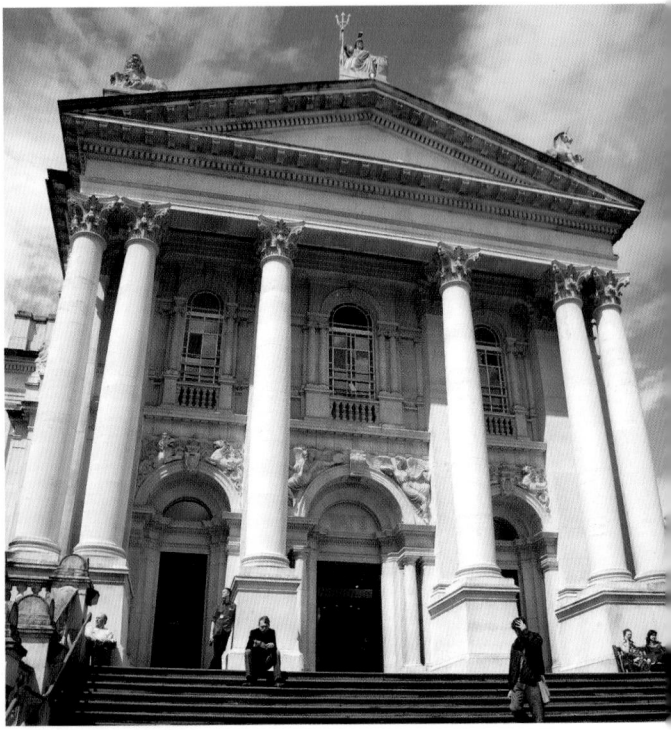

TOP 25

HIGHLIGHTS

- The Clore Gallery
- A Thomas Gainsborough portrait
- *Flatford Mill*, Constable
- A William Blake vision
- A William Hogarth caricature
- A Barbara Hepworth stone or wood sculpture
- A work on paper by David Hockney
- *The Opening of Waterloo Bridge*, Constable
- Temporary exhibitions
- The Tate-to-Tate ferry

With galleries rich in Gainsborough portraits, Turner landscapes, Hepworth sculptures and more, this is an intimate social history of Britain told by its artists.

The Gallery The Tate Gallery was opened in 1897, named after the millionaire Henry Tate, who paid for the core building and donated his Victorian pictures to it. The national collection, renamed Tate Britain after the modern art collection was moved to Tate Modern (▷ 54–55), remain in the original building on Millbank.

The Millbank Project This is a 20-year program of building works designed to transform the gallery. The first part, finished in 2013, upgraded the Millbank Entrance, Rotunda and some of the galleries.

Clockwise from far left: The imposing Millbank entrance to Tate Britain; paintings on display in the gallery; the rotunda dome, a masterpiece of Victorian architecture; the Turner Collection, the largest collection of works by J.M.W. Turner in the world, is housed in the modern Clore Gallery

British art The galleries are helpfully divided into four chronological suites. You can follow the visual story of British art from 1500 until the present day. Although paintings, sculptures, installations and works in other media are changed regularly, you may well see Van Dyck's lavish portraits of the 17th-century British aristocracy, William Hogarth's prints and richly colored Pre-Raphaelite canvases. Do not miss the great Turner collection housed in the adjoining Clore Gallery.

Turner Prize Britain's most prestigious and controversial prize to celebrate young British talent is run by the Tate and awarded each autumn. Founded in 1984, winners have included Damien Hurst, Grayson Perry, Duncan Campbell and Chris Ofili.

THE BASICS

www.tate.org.uk
J9
Millbank, SW1; entrances on Millbank and Atterbury Street
020 7887 8888
Daily 10–6
Restaurant, café
Pimlico, Vauxhall, Westminster
Vauxhall, Victoria
Very good
Free except for special exhibitions
Full education schedule; audio tours

21 Tate Modern

HIGHLIGHTS

- The dramatic Turbine Hall, the heart of the old power station
- Installation art
- Interactive digital projects
- The award-winning multimedia guides (small charge)

TIP

- The Tate Boat travels between Tate Modern and Tate Britain every 40 minutes during opening times.

The national collection of modern art fills the magnificent spaces of George Gilbert Scott's monumental Bankside Power Station by the Thames, making it a radical focus for the long strip of riverside arts emporia.

World-class art On a par with the Museum of Modern Art in New York, the collection that once shared space with the Tate's British collection (▷ 52–53) now blossoms in its own huge spaces. Swiss architects Herzog & de Meuron have created an exciting contemporary structure within the handsome brick building, making it ideal for exhibiting large-scale works of art. Gallery events, cafés, a big shop and a rooftop restaurant complete the total package for a great day on the South Bank. Alternatively combine traversing the innovative Millennium

Clockwise from far left: The monumental Turbine Hall, used for temporary exhibitions; the Millennium Bridge, linking Tate Modern with the City; a computer-generated image of the new extension to Tate Modern; The Kiss *(1901–04) by Auguste Rodin; Claude Monet's* Water-Lilies *(c.1916)*

Bridge, designed by Foster + Partners with Sir Anthony Caro, with city sightseeing.

20th century and more The most influential artists of the 20th century are all represented, including Picasso, Matisse, Dalí, Duchamp, Rodin, Klee and Warhol—as well as British artists such as Bacon, Hepworth, Hockney and Nicholson. Together they represent all the major periods and movements in 20th-century art. Suites of rooms, each devoted to one subject, mix together pieces from various periods.

Tate Modern project A striking new building rising behind the power station will transform the galleries. With 11 levels, it will double the space for displaying the collection and for installation and performance art.

THE BASICS

www.tate.org.uk
N6
Bankside, SE1
020 7887 8888
Sun–Thu 10–6, Fri–Sat 10–10. Closed 24–26 Dec
Cafés, restaurant
Blackfriars, Southwark
Blackfriars, London Bridge
Very good
Free, charge for some special exhibitions
Full educational schedule. Choice of free daily audio tours

22 Thames River Cruise

HIGHLIGHTS

- Lambeth Palace
- Houses of Parliament
- London Eye
- St. Paul's Cathedral
- Tower Bridge
- Tower of London
- Thames Barrier

TIPS

- Shop around for the best deals.
- The full circular tour takes about 1 hour.
- Take a jacket as London weather changes quickly.

A cruise along the Thames is a leisurely way to see the city. It gives a new perspective to London's development and history, which is inextricably linked with this great river.

Wonderful sights Many companies run river cruises and water-buses on the Thames. One particularly good stretch is from Westminster Pier in an easterly direction, which takes in a host of sights. This marks the point where the river enters central London and becomes a working highway, until recently lined with shipping, docks and warehouses. At this point the Thames flows between Lambeth Palace and the Houses of Parliament (▷ 22–23) and past the London Eye (▷ 30–31) and the Southbank Centre, making a northern loop past the Victoria Embankment and towards the

Clockwise from top left: A view over the Thames to St. Paul's Cathedral and the high-rises of the City; amphibious craft (DUKWs) provide tours with a difference (see panel, page 167); the landmark Tower Bridge; Big Ben and the Houses of Parliament; the Thames Flood Barrier

Millennium Bridge, linking St. Paul's Cathedral (▷ 44–45) and Tate Modern (▷ 54–55).

Great bridges Beyond Shakespeare's Globe (▷ 48–49) and Southwark Cathedral (▷ 74) the river reaches London Bridge, the modern crossing that replaced the 1831 version, itself replacing its arched medieval predecessor. The next crossing is Tower Bridge, designed to allow tall ships passage between the city and the sea. On the north bank is the Tower of London (▷ 58–59), William the Conqueror's fort placed strategically to protect the port.

Modern versus maritime From here the river passes the redeveloped Docklands. Seafaring is the theme as the Thames reaches Greenwich (▷ 20–21) and then the Thames Barrier.

THE BASICS

- K7
- Start point: Westminster Pier
- Westminster
- Moderate to expensive

Circular Cruise Westminster
020 7936 2033, www.crownrivercruise.co.uk

City Cruises
020 7740 0400, www.citycruises.com

Thames River Services
020 7930 4097, www.westminsterpier.co.uk

Westminster Passenger Service Association
020 7930 2062, www.wpsa.co.uk

23 Tower of London

TOP 25

HIGHLIGHTS

- Medieval Palace
- Raleigh's room
- Imperial State Crown
- Tower ravens
- Grand Punch Bowl, 1829
- St. John's Chapel

TIPS

- It's cheaper to buy tickets online at www.hrp.org.uk.
- If buying tickets on the day, it's vital to arrive early to avoid lines.

The superbly restored rooms of Edward I's 13th-century palace bring the Tower alive as the royal palace and place of pageantry it was. Don't miss gazing at the Crown Jewels.

Medieval glory The Tower of London is Britain's best medieval fortress. William the Conqueror (1066–87) began it as a show of brute force and Edward I (1272–1307) completed it. William's Caen stone White Tower, built within old Roman walls, was an excellent defence: It was 27m (90ft) high, with walls 4.5m (15ft) thick, and space for soldiers, servants and nobles. Henry III began the inner wall, the moat, his own watergate—and the royal zoo. Edward I built the outer wall, several towers and Traitor's Gate, and moved the Mint and Crown Jewels here.

Clockwise from far left: The mighty White Tower, begun by William the Conqueror in 1078; Waterloo Block, where the Crown Jewels are on display; historically, Yeoman Warders (known as Beefeaters), are the guardians of the Tower; Tower Green, former scene of private executions

Wonder and horror Stephen (1135–54) was the first king to live here, James I (1603–25) the last. From here Edward I went in procession to his coronation and Henry VIII paraded through the city bedecked in cloth of gold. The Barons seized the Tower to force King John to put his seal to the Magna Carta in 1215, and two princes were murdered while their uncle was being crowned Richard III. Since 1485 it has been guarded by Yeoman Warders or Beefeaters, who also now give guided tours.

Centuries of history The Tower has been a palace, fortress, state prison and execution site and its gates are still locked every night. If the history is overwhelming there is help in the shape of a welcome area, guided tours, an audio tour and numerous interactive displays.

THE BASICS

www.hrp.org.uk
S5
Tower Hill, EC3
Mar–Oct Tue–Sat 9–5.30, Sun–Mon 10–5.30; Nov–Feb Tue–Sat 9–4.30, Sun–Mon 10–4.30
Cafés, restaurant
Tower Hill
Fenchurch Street, London Bridge, Docklands Light Railway (Tower Gateway)
Excellent for Jewel House
Expensive
Free guided tours every 30 min; audio tours

24 Victoria and Albert Museum

HIGHLIGHTS

- British Galleries
- India and Islamic Galleries
- Jewellery Gallery
- Glass Gallery
- Leonardo da Vinci notebooks
- Silver collection
- Raphael Gallery
- Architecture Gallery
- The Hereford Screen

TIPS

- Hang out in the courtyard.
- Join a gallery tour or talk.
- Evening openings have a good atmosphere.

Part of the Victoria and Albert Museum's glory is that each room is unexpected—it may contain a French boudoir, plaster casts of classical sculptures, antique silver or exquisite contemporary glass.

A vision The V&A started as the South Kensington Museum. It was Prince Albert's vision—arts and science objects available to all people to inspire them to invent and create, with the accent on commercial design and craftsmanship. Since it opened in 1857, its collection, now comprising over a million works, has become so encyclopaedic, it ranks as the world's largest decorative arts museum.

Bigger and bigger Its size is unmanageable: 11km (7 miles) of gallery space on six floors.

Clockwise from left: The V&A, which opened in 1857, now ranks as the world's largest museum of decorative arts; exhibits in the museum's The Renaissance City 1350–1600 display; the Jameel Gallery, where exhibits showcase Islamic art from the eighth and ninth centuries

Its content is even more so—barely five percent of the 44,000 objects in the Indian department are on show. Larger museum objects include whole London house facades, grand rooms and the Raphael Cartoons. Despite this, contemporary work has been energetically bought and more than 60 percent of furniture entering the museum is 20th century.

Riches and rags Not every object in the museum is precious, and there are everyday things, unique pieces and opportunities to discover a fascination for a new subject—perhaps lace, ironwork, tiles or Japanese textiles. See the lavishly refurbished British and Whiteley Silver galleries, the magnificent collections in the Medieval and Renaissance galleries and the striking new Ceramics Gallery and Study Centre.

THE BASICS

www.vam.ac.uk
C8
Cromwell Road, SW7
020 7942 2000
Daily 10–5.45 (Fri 10–10). Closed 24–26 Dec
Restaurant, café
South Kensington
Very good
Free (except some special exhibitions)
Free daily guided, introductory tours. Talks, courses, demonstrations, workshops and concerts

25 Westminster Abbey

TOP 25

HIGHLIGHTS

- Poets' Corner
- Sir Isaac Newton memorial
- Sir James Thornhill's window
- Henry VII's Chapel
- Edward the Confessor's Chapel
- St. Faith's Chapel
- Grave of the Unknown Soldier
- Little Cloister and College Garden
- Weekday sung evensong at 5pm

TIPS

- Attend a service and hear the choirboys, accompanied by the abbey organ.
- Free organ recitals, Sun 5.45; summer organ festival (mid-Jul to mid-Aug).

The best time to be in the abbey is for the 8am service, sometimes held in St. Faith's Chapel. Follow this with a wander in the nave and cloisters before the crowds arrive.

The kernel of London's second city It was Edward the Confessor who in the 11th century began the rebuilding of the Benedictine abbey church of St. Peter, which was consecrated in 1065. The first sovereign to be crowned there was William the Conqueror in 1066. Successive kings were patrons, as were the pilgrims who flocked to the Confessor's shrine. Henry III (1216–72) employed Master Henry de Reyns to begin the Gothic abbey that stands today, and Henry VII (1485–1509) built his Tudor chapel with its delicate fan vaulting. Since William I, all sovereigns have been crowned

Clockwise from far left: The West Front; the Grave of the Unknown Soldier, adorned with Remembrance Day poppies; the shrine of Edward the Confessor, the abbey's founder; the choir stalls and ornate gilt altar; the abbey's magnificent vaulted ceiling

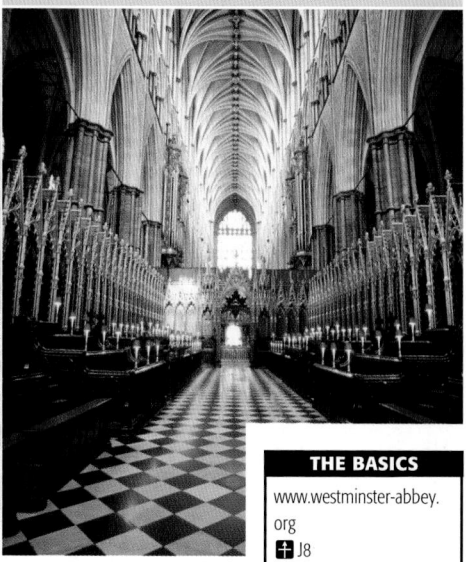

here—even after Henry VIII broke with Rome in 1533; and all were buried here up to George II (after which Windsor became the royal burial place, ▷ 79). It has also hosted 16 royal marriages, most recently that of Prince William and Catherine Middleton in 2011.

Daunting riches The abbey is massive, full of monuments, and very popular. From the nave's west end enjoy the view of the abbey, then look over the Victorian Gothic choir screen into Henry V's chantry. Having explored the chapels, the royal necropolis and Poets' Corner, leave time for the quiet cloister with superb views of the flying buttresses supporting the nave. In the abbey museum you can see macabre wax effigies, including those of Queen Elizabeth I and Lord Nelson, and a 13th-century altarpiece.

THE BASICS

www.westminster-abbey.org
J8
Broad Sanctuary, SW1; entry by North Door
020 7222 5152
Abbey: Mon–Sat times vary, call or check website; no photography. Abbey Museum, College Garden: daily various hours. Closed before special services, Sun, 24–25 Dec, Good Fri and Commonwealth Day
Westminster, St. James's Park
Victoria
Good
Expensive
Guided tours, audio guides

More to See

This section contains other great places to visit if you have more time. Some are in the heart of the city while others are a short journey away, found under Farther Afield. This chapter also has fantastic excursions that you should set aside a whole day to visit.

In the Heart of the City 66
30 St. Mary Axe 66
Albert Memorial 66
Apsley House (Wellington Museum) 66
Bank of England Museum 66
Borough Market 66
British Library 67
Brompton Oratory 67
Charles Dickens Museum 67
Churchill War Rooms 67
City Hall 68
Clarence House 68
Cleopatra's Needle 68
Covent Garden Piazza 69
Eros 69
Foundling Museum 69
Garden Museum 69
Golden Hinde II 69
Green Park 70
Guildhall Art Gallery 70
Handel House Museum 70
Hayward Gallery 70
HMS *Belfast* 70
Holy Trinity, Sloane Square 71
Hyde Park 71
Leadenhall Building 71
London Transport Museum 71
Madame Tussaud's 72
Peter Pan Statue 72
Petrie Museum 72
Photographers' Gallery 72
Regent's Park and ZSL London Zoo 72
Royal Academy of Arts 73
St. Bartholomew-the-Great 73
St. James's, Piccadilly 73
St. Katharine Docks 73
SEA LIFE London Aquarium 74
The Shard 74
Sir John Soane's Museum 74
Southwark Cathedral 74
Spencer House 75
Temple Church 75
Temple of Mithras 75
Trafalgar Square 75
Wallace Collection 75

Farther Afield 76
Canary Wharf 76
Chelsea Physic Garden 76
Chiswick House 76
Dulwich Picture Gallery 76
Firepower Museum 76
Ham House 76
Hampstead Heath 77
Jewish Museum 77
Kenwood House 77
Kew Gardens 77
London Wetland Centre 77
Museum of London Docklands 77
V&A Museum of Childhood 77
Whitechapel Art Gallery 77

Excursions 78
Hampton Court Palace 78
Windsor 79

In the Heart of the City

30 ST. MARY AXE

This landmark tower, designed by Foster + Partners and affectionately known as "The Gherkin," adds wit to the cluster of tall buildings in London's financial hub.

R4 30 St. Mary Axe, EC3 Not open to the general public Bank

ALBERT MEMORIAL

www.royalparks.org.uk

George Gilbert Scott's Gothic extravaganza, dedicated to Prince Albert, celebrates Victorian achievement with marble statues representing the Arts, Sciences, Industry and Continents. The finely carved frieze at its base depicts famous people in the Arts.

B7 Alexandra Gate, Kensington Gardens, SW7 South Kensington

APSLEY HOUSE (WELLINGTON MUSEUM)

www.english-heritage.org.uk

The splendid mansion was built for Arthur Wellesley, Duke of Wellington (1769–1852). The sumptuous interior houses his magnificent collection of paintings and decorative arts, with works by Velázquez and Rubens, as well as silver, porcelain and Canova's nude statue of Napoleon.

F7 Hyde Park Corner, W1 020 7499 5676 Apr–Oct Wed–Sun 11–5; Nov–Mar 11–4 Hyde Park Corner Moderate

BANK OF ENGLAND MUSEUM

www.bankofengland.co.uk/museum

Exhibits illustrate the history of Britain's monetary and banking system since 1694. Take time to appreciate the re-creations of Soane's rooms and Sir Herbert Baker's Rotunda. The museum stages changing exhibitions.

Q4 Bartholomew Lane, EC2 020 7601 5545 Mon–Fri 10–5, last admission 4.45 Bank Free

BOROUGH MARKET

www.boroughmarket.org.uk

Top quality British and international produce is offered at London's oldest and most exciting food market. Many of the traders are artisan producers, keen to share their passion for good food and

The glittering Albert Memorial and nearby Albert Hall

30 St. Mary Axe, dubbed "The Gherkin"

fine ingredients. Good restaurants and trendy cafés complete the attractive scene.

Q6 Southwark Street, SE1 Wed–Thu 10–5, Fri 10–6, Sat 8–5 (lunch only Mon–Tue 10–5) London Bridge London Bridge

BRITISH LIBRARY

www.bl.uk

The library is home to well over150 million items in most known languages, including maps, manuscripts, prints, drawings, music scores, patents, sound recordings and eight million stamps. Among its many treasures are a 1215 copy of the Magna Carta, original editions of Chaucer's *Canterbury Tales*, the Gutenberg Bible, Shakespeare's first folio, Handel's *Messiah*, Beatles' manuscripts, Leonardo da Vinci's notebook and Captain Scott's diary of his ill-fated Antarctic expedition.

J1 96 Euston Road, NW1 Mon–Thu 9.30–8, Fri 9.30–6, Sat 9.30–5, Sun 11–5 Café, restaurant King's Cross, St Pancras Free; charge for special events and exhibitions

BROMPTON ORATORY

www.bromptonoratory.com

Standing next door to the V&A, the flamboyant Oratory of St. Philip Neri was built in 1884 and given a sumptuous, sculpture-filled interior.

C8 Brompton Road, SW7 020 7808 0900 Daily 6.30am–8pm South Kensington Donation

CHARLES DICKENS MUSEUM

www.dickensmuseum.com

Visit the house where Dickens wrote his novels *Nicholas Nickleby* and *Oliver Twist*. A £3.1 million restoration project has given visitors a real sense of his life and work.

L2 48 Doughty Street, WC1 020 7405 2127 Daily 10–5, last admission 4 Café Russell Square Moderate

CHURCHILL WAR ROOMS

www.iwm.org.uk

Britain's war effort was directed from these secret rooms in a bunker complex hidden beneath Whitehall 's streets. The Cabinet War Rooms, where Churchill and his War Cabinet met, offices and

Fresh seafood at Borough Market

The British Library piazza, with Eduardo Paolozzi's bronze statue

dormitories reveal what life was like underground for the hundreds of staff while bombs rained overhead. The Map Room is exactly how it was left when the lights were switched off in August 1945. Interactive displays in the Churchill Museum explore his fascinating life and legacy with personal letters, extracts from speeches, historic documents, photos and film clips.

J7 Clive Steps, King Charles Street, SW1 020 7930 6961 Daily 9.30–6 (last admission 5) St. James's Park, Westminster Expensive

CITY HALL

www.london.gov.uk

Architect Sir Norman Foster's distinctive glass building is the office of the Mayor of London and the capital's governing body, the London Assembly. The highlight of any visit is to climb the clear 500m (1,640ft) helical staircase, winding up through all ten storys, to a viewing deck at the top. The Scoop, an outdoor amphitheatre, seats 800 for summer events.

R6 The Queen's Walk, SE1 020 7983 4000 Mon–Thu 8.30–6, Fri 8.30–5.30 London Bridge Free

CLARENCE HOUSE

www.royalcollection.org.uk

Built for Prince William, Duke of Clarence and later William IV, this was the late Queen Mother's London home, now magnificently renovated by its current resident, the Prince of Wales. Five rooms used by Prince Charles and the Duchess of Cornwall for official engagements can be seen. All tickets are timed and must be prebooked.

H7 Off the Mall, SW1 020 7766 7303 Guided tours Aug Mon–Fri 10–4.30, Sat–Sun 10–5.30 St. James's Park, Green Park Moderate

CLEOPATRA'S NEEDLE

This impressive 26m (86ft) pink granite obelisk was constructed in Ancient Egypt in 1450BC and records the triumphs of Rameses the Great.

K6 Victoria Embankment, WC2 Embankment, Charing Cross Free

City Hall, home to the Greater London Authority

COVENT GARDEN PIAZZA

www.coventgardenlondonuk.com

London's first square was laid out in the 1630s by architect Inigo Jones. It later became a fruit and vegetable market. Redeveloped in the 1980s, the piazza is a popular meeting and eating place, with lively street entertainment.

H5 Cafés, restaurants and bars
Covent Garden

EROS

Alfred Gilbert's memorial (1893) to the philanthropic 7th Earl of Shaftesbury (1801–85), *The Angel of Christian Charity*, is popularly referred to as Eros, although it actually depicts Anteros, the god of selfless love.

H5 Piccadilly Circus, W1
Piccadilly Circus

FOUNDLING MUSEUM

www.foundlingmuseum.org.uk

When Thomas Coran founded a hospice for abandoned children in 1739, Handel and Hogarth helped to raise funds. Both the building and the art, which includes paintings by Gainsborough, Hogarth and Millais, are magnificent. The Gerald Coke Handel Collection has amazing material relating to the composer and his contemporaries.

K2 40 Brunswick Square, WC1
020 7841 3600 Tue–Sat 10–5, Sun 11–5. Closed 23–26 Dec, 1 Jan Café
Russell Square Moderate

GARDEN MUSEUM

www.gardenmuseum.org.uk

Celebrating the plant-hunting Tradescants and 400 years of garden and plant history in an old church, knot garden and gallery.

L8 Lambeth Palace Road, SE1
020 7401 8865 Daily 10.30–5 (Sat 4), closed 1st Mon of month
Café Lambeth North
Moderate

GOLDEN HINDE II

www.goldenhinde.com

The ship is an exact replica of the 16th-century galleon in which Sir Francis Drake circumnavigated the globe. Take a look at the website for events and tours.

A street performer entertains the crowds at Covent Garden Piazza

Eros, at the heart of Piccadilly Circus

Q6 St. Mary Overie Dock, Cathedral Street, SE1 020 7403 0123 Usually daily 10–5.30, but hours vary
Refreshment kiosks London Bridge
London Bridge Moderate

GREEN PARK

www.royalparks.org.uk

Covering 19ha (47 acres), Green Park is a popular venue for summer picnics, and famous for its mature trees, tree-lined avenues, grass lawns and attractive spring daffodil displays.

G7 SW1 0300 061 2350
Daily 24 hrs Green Park, Hyde Park Corner Free

GUILDHALL ART GALLERY

www.cityoflondon.gov.uk

The gallery offers two remarkable things to see: the Guildhall's quirky collection of mostly British pictures, and part of Roman London's huge amphitheater, built in AD200 and rediscovered in 1988. Stop to admire the Guildhall yard too.

P4 Guildhall Yard, Gresham Street, EC2 020 7332 3700 Mon–Sat 10–5, Sun 12–4 St. Paul's, Bank Free

HANDEL HOUSE MUSEUM

www.handelhouse.org

Anyone who plays an instrument or sings *The Messiah* should visit the composer's London home from 1723 until 1759. There are weekly concerts and events.

G5 25 Brook Street, W1 020 7495 1685 Tue–Wed, Fri–Sat 10–6, Thu 10–8, Sun 12–6 Bond Street, Oxford Circus Moderate

HAYWARD GALLERY

www.southbankcentre.co.uk

Housed in a brutalist-style buildings from the 1960s, the Hayward stages work by pioneering artists. Concrete is a day café that morphs into a night bar with DJs and an eclectic playlist.

L6 Belvedere Road, SE1
Mon 12–6; Tue–Wed, Sat–Sun 11–7, Thu–Fri 11–8 during exhibitions
Waterloo Waterloo Moderate–expensive; some exhibitions free

HMS *BELFAST*

www.iwm.org.uk

Clamber up, down and around this 1938 war cruiser, visiting the

The retired 1938 war cruiser HMS Belfast

cabins, gun turrets, dining hall, bridge and boiler-room to get a taste of life onboard a warship.
R6 The Queen's Walk, SE1 020 7940 6300 Mar–Oct daily 10–6; Nov–Feb 10–5 Café London Bridge London Bridge Expensive

HOLY TRINITY, SLOANE SQUARE

www.holytrinitysloanesquare.co.uk
London's best Arts and Crafts church, designed by J.D. Sedding, has glass by Burne-Jones, William Morris and others. Note the huge east window with its 48 panels depicting saints.
E9 Sloane Square, SW1 020 7730 7270 Mon–Sat 8.30–5.30, Sun 8.30–1.30 Sloane Square Donation

HYDE PARK

www.royalparks.org.uk
One of city's largest open spaces, the park was tamed in the 18th century, it is the perfect place for a picnic. Don't miss the views from the Serpentine Bridge, the Rose Garden or the Diana, Princess of Wales Memorial Fountain.
E6 W2 0300 061 2000 Daily 5am–midnight Restaurant, café Knightsbridge, Lancaster Gate Hyde Park Corner Free

LEADENHALL BUILDING

www.theleadenhallbuilding.com
Nicknamed the "Cheesegrater," London's newest skyscraper, at 224m (734ft) the tallest in the City's financial district, is a stunning glass and steel construction designed by Richard Rogers.
R4 122 Leadenhall Street, EC3 Limited public access Bank

LONDON TRANSPORT MUSEUM

www.ltmuseum.co.uk
With beautifully restored old buses, trams, trolleybuses and underground rail vehicles, themed galleries tell the story of London's transport system and 200 years of social history.
K5 Covent Garden Piazza, WC2 020 7379 6344 Sat–Thu 10–6, Fri 11–6 Café Covent Garden Charing Cross Expensive; free for under 17s

The Diana, Princess of Wales Memorial Fountain, Hyde Park

MADAME TUSSAUD'S

www.madametussauds.com/London

See how many famous people you can identify, from Shakespeare to Prince Harry and the Beckhams.

E3 Marylebone Road, NW1 Hours vary, check website for details Café Baker Street Expensive; family ticket

PETER PAN STATUE

George Frampton's statue (1912) commemorating J.M. Barrie's fictional creation, the boy who never grew up, stands in Kensington Gardens.

B6 Long Water, Kensington Gardens Lancaster Gate

PETRIE MUSEUM

www.ucl.ac.uk/museums/petrie

The ancient spoils of many Egyptologists' explorations are on display at the hard-to-find Petrie Museum (it's close to the rear of the British Museum). With 80,000 objects, it's one of the world's greatest collections of Egyptian and Sudanese archaeology.

J2 Univeristy College London, Malet Place, WC1 020 7679 2884 Tue–Sat 1–5 Euston Square Free

PHOTOGRAPHERS' GALLERY

http://thephotographersgallery.org.uk

An £8.7-million project has transformed an Edwardian warehouse into a state-of-the-art home for the Photographers' Gallery. The gallery has three floors of exhibition space, a bookshop and café, and hosts a range of talks and events (check website for details).

H4 16–18 Ramillies Street, W1 020 7087 9300 Mon–Sat 10–6, Thu to 8, Sun 11.30–6 Oxford Circus Inexpensive; free Mon–Fri 10–12 and for under 16s

REGENT'S PARK AND ZSL LONDON ZOO

www.royalparks.org.uk; www.zsl.org

Regent's Park has vast rose gardens, a boating lake, sports facilities and an open-air theater in the summer. London Zoo, in its northeastern corner, is popular with children and offers activities during holidays.

The London Transport Museum celebrates the capital's transport system

Wax figures at Madame Tussaud's

Off map at D1–F1 Outer Circle, Regent's Park, NW1 Park: 0300 061 2300. Zoo: 020 7722 3333 Park: daily from 5am. Zoo: from 10. Closing times change seasonally Cafés Regent's Park, Camden Town Park: Free. Zoo: Expensive

ROYAL ACADEMY OF ARTS

www.royalacademy.org.uk

The Royal Academy hosts major art shows, plus the annual Summer Exhibition, held every year since 1769. Don't miss the rooftop Sackler Galleries.

H5 Burlington House, Piccadilly, W1 020 7300 8000 Sat–Thu 10–6, Fri 10–10 Restaurant, café Green Park, Piccadilly Circus Expensive

ST. BARTHOLOMEW-THE-GREAT

www.greatstbarts.com

Built in 1123, this is the City's only 12th-century monastic church, and its best surviving piece of Romanesque architecture.

N3 West Smithfield, EC1 020 7600 0440 Mon–Fri 8.30–5 (4pm mid-Nov to mid-Feb), Sat 10.30–4, Sun 8.30–8. Sun services at 9, 11, 6.30 Café Barbican, Farringdon, St. Paul's Farringdon Inexpensive

ST. JAMES'S, PICCADILLY

www.sjp.org.uk

Wren's church (1682–84), built for the local aristocracy, has a sumptuous interior. Some superb concerts are held here (check website for details) and the courtyard hosts market stalls.

H6 197 Piccadilly, W1 020 7734 4511 Daily 8–6.30 Café Piccadilly Circus Donation

ST. KATHARINE DOCKS

www.skdocks.co.uk

Luxury yachts now fill the marina close to Tower Bridge where cargoes were once landed, while restaurants, bars, shops and apartments fill the former warehouses. Explore the international Good Food Market at Marble Quay on Friday lunchtimes.

S6 St. Katharine's Way, E1 020 7488 0555 Tower Hill Tower Gateway (DLR), Fenchurch Street Tower Pier, St. Katharine's Pier Free

The Royal Academy of Arts

A titi monkey, one of the inhabitants of ZSL London Zoo

SEA LIFE LONDON AQUARIUM

www.visitsealife.com/london

More than 3,000 forms of marine life, including sharks, stingrays and turtles, fill this aquatic spectacular.

L7 County Hall, SE1 Daily 10–7 Westminster, Waterloo Expensive

THE SHARD

www.theviewfromtheshard.com

Occupying floors 68–72 of The Shard, London's tallest landmark shimmering 310m (1,016ft) skywards, The View offers uninterrupted 360-degree panoramics across the capital and beyond.

R6 Joiner Street, SE1 0344 499 7111 Apr–Oct daily 10–10; Nov–Mar Sun–Wed 10–7, Thu–Sat 10–10. Last entry 90 minutes before closing. Timed tickets, pre-booking advised London Bridge London Bridge Expensive

SIR JOHN SOANE'S MUSEUM

www.soane.org

The gloriously overfurnished home of neo-classical architect and avid collector Sir John Soane is a treasure trove of surprises. Canaletto's paintings hang in the breakfast room, Hogarth's unfold from the walls, and there's even an Egyptian pharaoh's sarcophagus downstairs. Acquired between the 1780s and his death in 1837, there are so many sculptures, paintings and antiquities packing every surface that unless you keep your eyes peeled you are likely to miss a Watteau drawing or something better.

L4 13 Lincoln's Inn Fields, WC2 020 7405 2107 Tue–Sat 10–5. Last entry 4.30 Café London Bridge Holborn Free, donation

SOUTHWARK CATHEDRAL

http://cathedral.southwark.anglican.org

The fine stone building is powerfully atmospheric of its medieval origins, despite much rebuilding. Inside, there are fine choir stalls and some interesting monuments.

Q6 London Bridge, SE1 020 7367 6700 Mon–Fri 8–6, Sat–Sun 8.30–6 Café London Bridge London Bridge Donation

Southwark Cathedral retains a medieval appearance despite much rebuilding

Temple Church in the Inns of Court

SPENCER HOUSE

www.spencerhouse.co.uk

A lavishly restored Palladian mansion, Spencer House is a rare survivor of 18th-century aristocratic St. James's and Mayfair. Eight rooms with gilded decorations, period paintings and furniture are open to the public, along with the authentically restored garden.

H6 27 St. James's Place, SW1 020 7499 8620 Sun 10.30–4.45 (last tour). Closed Jan and Aug. Guided tours only Green Park Expensive; no children under 10

TEMPLE CHURCH

www.templechurch.com

Begun about 1160, this private chapel, built by the Knights Templar to a circular plan, stands at the heart of the Inns of Court. You can visit the Temple gardens and the 16th-century Middle Temple Hall. The church hosts fine music and organ recitals; check the website for details.

M4 Temple, EC4 020 7353 3470 Opening times vary, check website. Sun services Temple Inexpensive

TEMPLE OF MITHRAS

The Roman temple foundations of AD240–50 testify to the cult of the Persian god Mithras.

P5 Temple Court, Queen Victoria Street, EC4 Mansion House, Bank

TRAFALGAR SQUARE

Sir Edwin Landseer's lions protect Nelson's Column, erected to commemorate the 1805 Battle of Trafalgar, at the heart of this iconic square. The fountains were added in 1845. Bronze statues occupy three of the plinths; the fourth hosts changing works by contemporary artists.

J6 Restaurants and cafés Charing Cross Charing Cross Free

WALLACE COLLECTION

www.wallacecollection.org

French 18th-century paintings, Old Masters, furniture, porcelain and a world-class armory are all housed in a historic London town house.

F4 Hertford House, Manchester Square, W1 020 7563 9500 Daily 10–5 Restaurant, café Marble Arch, Bond Street Free

Bustling Trafalgar Square, a popular meeting place

Farther Afield

CANARY WHARF

www.canarywharf.com

César Pelli's soaring, pyramid-topped tower (1991) dominates the premier business district.

See page ▷ 115 1 Canada Square, Canary Wharf, E14 Public spaces are open, not buildings Canary Wharf

CHELSEA PHYSIC GARDEN

www.chelseaphysicgarden.co.uk

This 17th-century walled garden was laid out by Sir Hans Sloane for the Society of Apothecaries.

See page ▷ 114 66 Royal Hospital Road, SW3 020 7352 5646 Apr–Oct Tue–Fri, Sun 11–6 Café Sloane Square Moderate

CHISWICK HOUSE

www.chgt.org.uk

Lord Burlington's exquisite country villa (1725–29) has superb formal gardens and conservatories.

See page ▷ 114 Burlington Lane, W4 020 8995 0508 House: Apr–Oct Sun–Wed 10–5; Nov–Dec pre-booked tours only. Garden: daily 7–dusk Café Turnham Green Chiswick House: Moderate. Garden: Free

DULWICH PICTURE GALLERY

www.dulwichpicturegallery.org.uk

Opened in 1814, this was England's first public art gallery.

See page ▷ 115 Gallery Road, SE21 020 8693 5254 Tue–Fri 10–5, Sat–Sun 11–5 Café North or West Dulwich Moderate

FIREPOWER MUSEUM

www.firepower.org.uk

Exhibits here range from Roman trebuchets to an Iraqi supergun, with plenty of visitor participation.

See page ▷ 115 The Royal Arsenal, Woolwich, SE18 020 8855 7755 Tue–Sat 10–5 Café Woolwich Arsenal Ferry from Greenwich Moderate

HAM HOUSE

www.nationaltrust.org.uk

The house and garden at this Thameside baroque mansion have been meticulously restored.

See page ▷ 114 Ham, Richmond, Surrey, TW10 020 8940 1950 House: Mar–Oct Sat–Thu 12–4. Gardens: Daily 11–5 Café Richmond, then bus 371 Expensive

Historic Ham House and gardens, built in 1610 on the banks of the Thames

The Museum of London Docklands

HAMPSTEAD HEATH

www.cityoflondon.gov.uk

Hampstead Heath offers 325ha (800 acres) of open countryside to enjoy in north London.

See page ▷ 114 Hampstead, NW3 020 7482 7073 for visitor information Daily 7.30am–dusk Hampstead Free

JEWISH MUSEUM

www.jewishmuseum.org.uk

Exhibitions and activities on Jewish history, culture and heritage.

See page ▷ 114 129–131 Albert Street, NW1 020 7284 7384 Sat–Thu 10–5, Fri 10–2 Kosher café Camden Town Moderate

KENWOOD HOUSE

www.english-heritage.org.uk

Restyled by Robert Adam, this country house lies outside pretty Hampstead village in north London. Its walls are hung with Rembrandts, Romneys, Vermeers and Gainsboroughs and its landscaped parkland provides grand views. In summer, evening concerts are held in the grounds.

See page ▷ 114 Hampstead Lane, NW3 020 8348 1286 Daily 10–5 Café Hampstead Heath Free

KEW GARDENS

www.kew.org

With 44,000 plants and some glorious glasshouses, the 120ha (300-acre) Royal Botanic Gardens at Kew is a magical place. Walks on tree-shaded avenues, mesmerizing flower displays, a treetop walkway for bird's-eye views and the restored Kew Palace are just some of the attractions.

See page ▷ 114 Queen Elizabeth's Walk, SW13 020 8332 5655 Daily from 9.30, see website for closing times Café Kew Gardens, then bus 283 Richmond, then bus 65 Expensive

LONDON WETLAND CENTRE

www.wwt.org.uk

The Wildfowl and Wetlands Trust administers 42ha (104 acres) of lakes, ponds, grassland and mudflats that attract a variety of wildlife.

See page ▷ 114 Queen Elizabeth's Walk, SW13 020 8409 4400 Apr–Oct daily 9.30–6; Nov–Mar 9.30–5 Café Hammersmith, then bus 283 Barnes, then bus 33, 72 Expensive

MUSEUM OF LONDON DOCKLANDS

www.museumoflondon.org.uk/docklands

The museum tells the story of London's river, port and people from Roman times until now. It also hosts events and tours.

See page ▷ 115 No. 1 Warehouse, West India Quay, Canary Wharf, E14 020 7001 9844 Daily 10–6 Restaurant West India Quay, Canary Wharf Free

V&A MUSEUM OF CHILDHOOD

www.vam.ac.uk/moc

Exhibits here explore playtime from 1600 to the present day, with Noah's arks, dolls, toy soldiers and even a model circus.

See page ▷ 115 Cambridge Heath Road, E2 020 8983 5200 Daily 10–5.45 Café Bethnal Green Bethnal Green Free

WHITECHAPEL ART GALLERY

www.whitechapelgallery.org

Influential hub of the East End contemporary art activities (▷ 6–7).

S4 77–82 Whitechapel High Street, E1 020 7522 7888 Tue–Wed, Fri–Sun 11–6, Thu 11–9 Café Aldgate East Free

HAMPTON COURT PALACE

www.hrp.org.uk

This is London's most impressive royal palace, well worth the 35-minute train journey out from central London.

When King Henry VIII dismissed Cardinal Wolsey in 1529, he took over his already ostentatious Tudor palace and enlarged it. Successive monarchs altered and repaired both the palace and its 12ha (29 acres) of Tudor and baroque gardens.

The best way to visit this huge collection of chambers, courtyards and state apartments is to follow one of the six clearly indicated routes—perhaps Henry VIII's State Apartments or the King's Apartments built for William III, immaculately restored after a devastating fire. Highlights include Henry VIII's Great Hall, which is recognized as England's finest medieval hall. William Shakespeare performed plays here between 1603 and 1604. The Chapel Royal, still in use after 450 years, should not to be missed. Neither should the vast Tudor kitchens, built to feed Henry VIII's court, providing over 600 meals twice a day. Live cookery demonstrations are given every month; check the website for dates of these and other events.

You can easily spend a day at the palace, but allow at least three hours for your visit. Do not miss the formal Tudor gardens that reach down to the River Thames, the famous Maze and restored Privy Garden, looking now as it would have done when it was created for William III in 1702.

Children love Hampton Court, not least because there are so many events and activities designed especially for them, including costumed presentations and family audio guides and trails.

Distance: 16km (10 miles)
Journey time: 35 min
East Molesey, Surrey
Apr–Oct daily 10–6; Nov–Mar 10–4.30
Café, restaurant Waterloo to Hampton Court Riverboat to Hampton Court Expensive

The beautiful formal flower gardens at Hampton Court Palace

The palace's courtyard and entrance gate

WINDSOR

www.windsor.gov.uk
www.royalcollection.org.uk

Fairy-tale towers and turrets make this the ultimate royal castle. An official residence of Her Majesty the Queen, it's the oldest and largest occupied castle in the world. As it is a working royal palace, opening times can change, so check the website for the latest information.

Begun by William the Conqueror and rebuilt in stone by Henry II, the castle has been embellished over the centuries. The richly decorated State Apartments are hung with paintings by Old Masters. The tombs of 10 sovereigns, including Henry VIII and Charles I, lie amid the fine Gothic architecture of St. George's Chapel, setting for the service of dedication following the marriage of Prince Charles and the Duchess of Cornwall in 2005.

Should the State Apartments or Chapel be closed, there is still much to see. The Drawings Gallery has changing exhibitions, and don't miss Queen Mary's Dolls' House, designed by Edward Lutyens. Some 1,500 craftspeople were involved in its construction.

Changing the Guard takes place at 11am daily, April to the end of July, and on alternate days for the rest of the year, weather permitting, but never on Sundays.

Outside the castle lie Windsor's medieval cobblestoned lanes, Christopher Wren's Guildhall and the Theatre Royal. Beyond it, you can explore 1,950ha (4,700-acre) Windsor Great Park and cross the river footbridge to Eton.

Distance: 37km (23 miles)
Journey time: 40–55 min

Windsor Tourist Information

✉ Windsor Royal Shopping, Thames Street ☎ 01753 743900 ⏲ Daily Jan–Feb, Nov–Dec 9.45–4.15; Mar–Oct 9.45–5.15 (last admission 1hr 15 min before closing) 🚆 Waterloo to Windsor & Eton Riverside, Paddington to Windsor & Eton Central

Windsor Castle

☎ 01753 831118 ⏲ Apr–May Mon–Sat 10–5, Sun 10–4; Jun–Oct Mon–Sat 9.30–5, Sun–10-4; Nov–Mar Sun–Fri 10-4, Sat 10–5 (last admission 75 minutes before closing) £ Expensive

Stately Windsor Castle

Great Park and the Long Walk entrance to Windsor Castle

Pavilion End
Pavilion End
The BIG BACK FOUR

City Tours

This section contains self-guided tours that will help you explore the sights in each of the city's regions. Each tour is designed to take a day, with a map pinpointing the recommended places along the way. There is a quick reference guide at the end of each tour, listing everything you need in that region, so you know exactly what's close by.

South Bank	**82**
Fleet Street to the Tower	**88**
Covent Garden to Regent's Park	**94**
Westminster and St. James's	**100**
Around Hyde Park	**106**
Farther Afield	**112**

South Bank

With mesmerizing river views, exciting contemporary art at Tate Modern, medieval history at Southwark Cathedral, world-class concert halls and a theatrical tradition dating back to Shakespeare's time, the South Bank has plenty to entice visitors.

Morning
Start at **Tower Bridge** and set the scene for your day with high-level, panoramic views, spotting London's tallest landmark, **The Shard** (▷ 74). Then stroll among the converted warehouses of Shad Thames, home to numerous shops and cafés. Join the well-signed riverside Thames Path, passing the distinctive **City Hall** (▷ 68), seat of government, and the moored war cruiser **HMS *Belfast*** (right, ▷ 70).

Mid-morning
From Tooley Street, zigzag under **London Bridge** to visit **Southwark Cathedral** (left, ▷ 74). Admire the soaring nave, choir and 16th-century Great Screen, and look for stained-glass windows depicting famous Southwark inhabitants, including Chaucer and Shakespeare. The **Harvard Chapel** reveals some of the cathedral's many links with America.

Lunch
Borough Market (right, ▷ 67) is nearby and the perfect location for lunch, especially Wednesdays to Saturdays when it is packed with enticing food stalls and the restaurants are particularly lively.

Afternoon
Return to the riverside, passing the fine 14th-century rose window in the ruins of **Winchester Palace**, to see the replica of Sir Francis Drake's magnificent galleon, *Golden Hinde II* (right, ▷ 69). Walk through medieval Clink Street, once the site of a notorious prison. Passing under Southwark Bridge, restaurants, cafés and pubs with river views line the route to **Shakespeare's Globe** (▷ 48–49), a faithful reconstruction of an Elizabethan open-air theater. The excellent guided tour of the theater is not to be missed.

Mid-afternoon
Explore the contemporary art at **Tate Modern** (▷ 54–55) and take time for tea in its café with a view. Continue your stroll along the Thames Path, enjoying views of the architecture lining the opposite bank of the river. Have a look in the crafts studios on the lower floors of the **Oxo Tower** (left) and in nearby **Gabriel's Wharf**, before you reach **Waterloo Bridge**—you may find a secondhand books market under its arches—and the **Southbank Centre**.

Dinner
There's a vast choice of restaurants around here, but if you're up for somewhere smart with unmatched views, book a table at the **Oxo Tower Bar, Brasserie and Restaurant** (▷ 149).

Evening
With concerts by world-class musicians at the **Royal Festival Hall** (▷ 138), plays at the **National Theatre** (▷ 136) and films at **BFI Southbank** (▷ 133), you're spoiled for choice for entertainment in this part of London. Free live music events are often held in the early evening. Alternatively, a ride on the **London Eye** (▷ 30) at night is a magical experience.

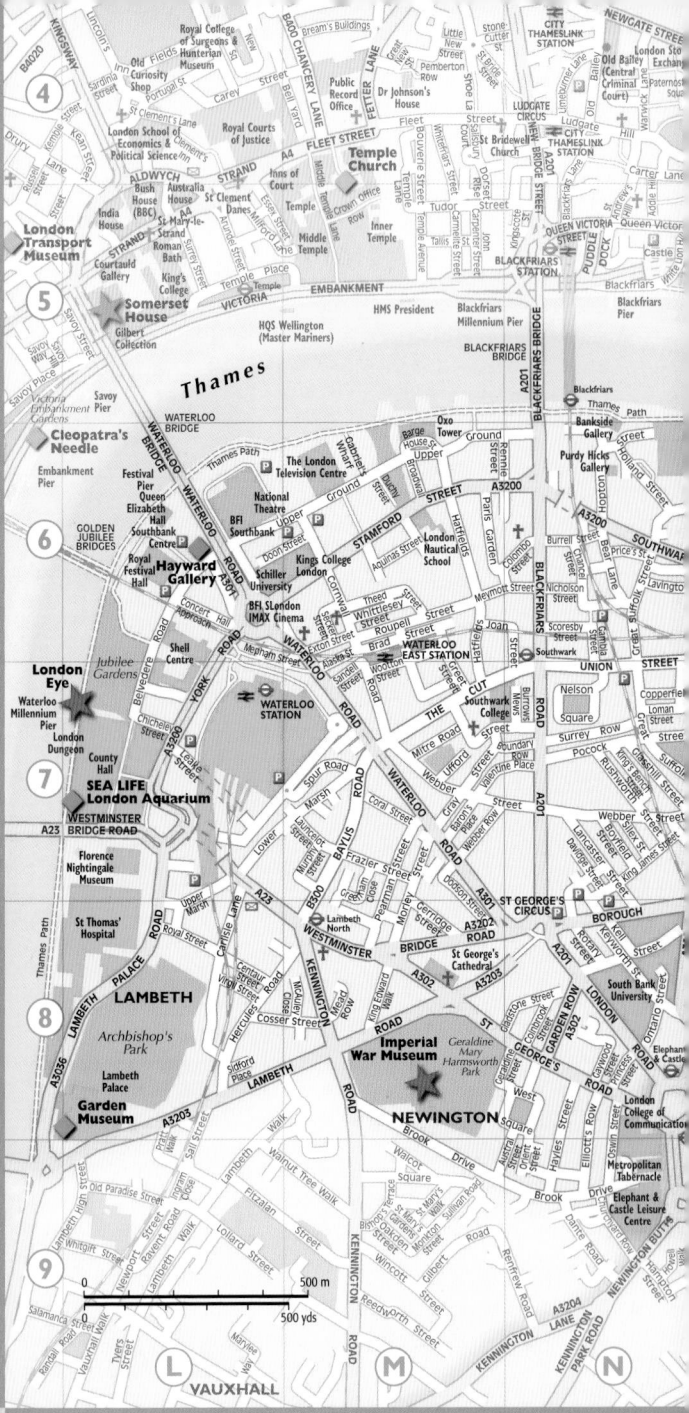
Thames
Temple Church
London Transport Museum
Somerset House
Cleopatra's Needle
Hayward Gallery
London Eye
SEA LIFE London Aquarium
LAMBETH
Garden Museum
Imperial War Museum
NEWINGTON
VAUXHALL
Royal College of Surgeons & Hunterian Museum
Old Curiosity Shop
Royal Courts of Justice
Public Record Office
Dr Johnson's House
CITY THAMESLINK STATION
Old Bailey (Central Criminal Court)
St Bridewell Church
Inns of Court
Middle Temple
Inner Temple
Royal Festival Hall
Shell Centre
WATERLOO STATION
WATERLOO EAST STATION
Southwark
Southwark College
Florence Nightingale Museum
St Thomas' Hospital
Lambeth Palace
Lambeth North
St George's Cathedral
ST GEORGE'S CIRCUS
South Bank University
Metropolitan Tabernacle
Elephant & Castle Leisure Centre
London College of Communication
Purdy Hicks Gallery
Bankside Gallery
Oxo Tower
The London Television Centre
National Theatre
BFI Southbank
BFI London IMAX Cinema
Kings College London
Schiller University
London Nautical School
Somerset House
HMS President
Blackfriars Millennium Pier
HQS Wellington (Master Mariners)
Gilbert Collection
Courtauld Gallery
King's College
Australia House
India House
Bush House (BBC)
St Clement Danes
St Mary-le-Strand
Roman Bath
Royal College of Surgeons & Hunterian Museum
Embankment Pier
Festival Pier
Queen Elizabeth Hall
Southbank Centre
GOLDEN JUBILEE BRIDGES
Waterloo Millennium Pier
London Dungeon
County Hall
WESTMINSTER BRIDGE ROAD
Jubilee Gardens
Victoria Embankment Gardens
Savoy Pier
Lambeth Palace
Archbishop's Park
Geraldine Mary Harrmsworth Park
Nelson Square
Blackfriars Pier
Blackfriars Station
Blackfriars Bridge
Waterloo Bridge
Westminster Bridge
Lambeth Bridge
Vauxhall Bridge
Kew Bridge
Hampton Court Bridge
Thames Path
0 500 m
0 500 yds
L
M
N

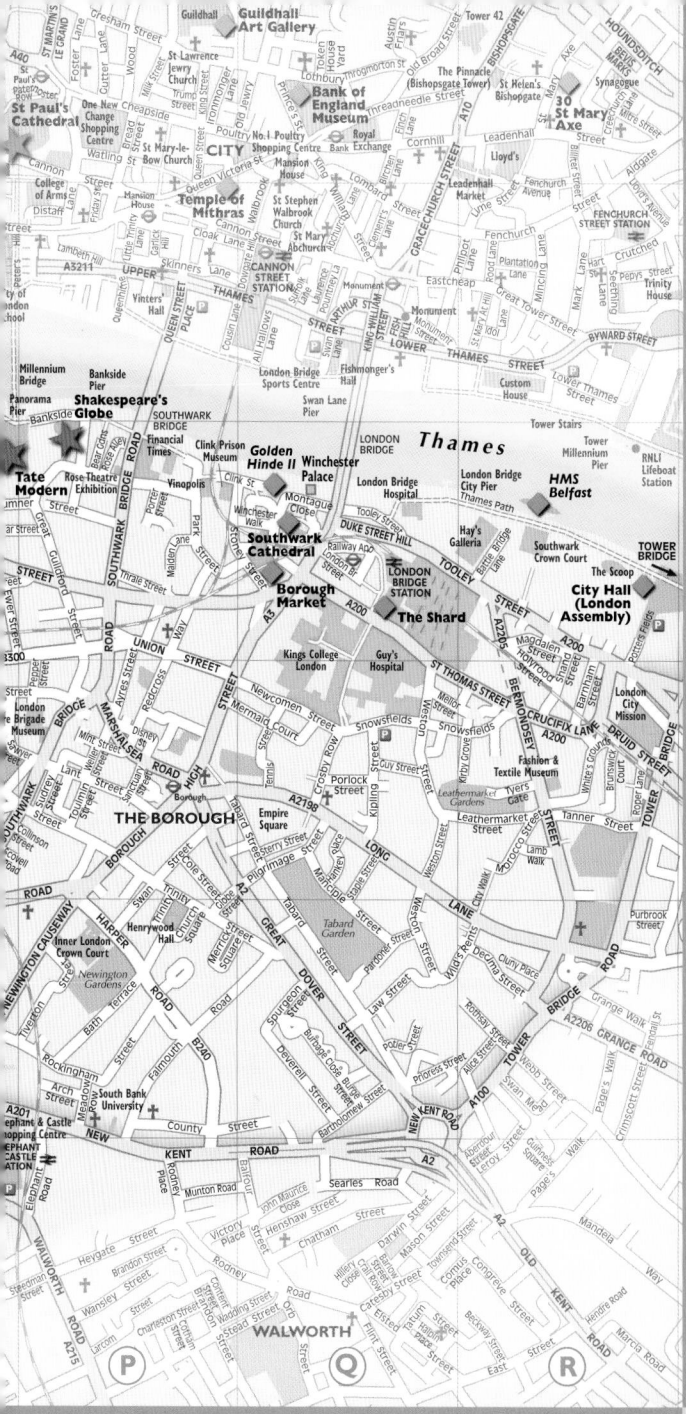
Guildhall Art Gallery
Guildhall
Tower 42
St Paul's Cathedral
Bank of England Museum
The Pinnacle (Bishopsgate Tower)
St Helen's Bishopgate
30 St Mary Axe
Synagogue
CITY
Royal Exchange
Mansion House
Temple of Mithras
St Stephen Walbrook Church
St Mary Abchurch
Lloyd's
Leadenhall Market
GRACECHURCH STREET
FENCHURCH STREET STATION
CANNON STREET STATION
Monument
Eastcheap
Great Tower Street
BYWARD STREET
LOWER THAMES STREET
Trinity House
Millennium Bridge
Bankside Pier
Panorama Pier
Shakespeare's Globe
SOUTHWARK BRIDGE
Financial Times
Clink Prison Museum
Golden Hinde II
Winchester Palace
LONDON BRIDGE
Thames
Tower Millennium Pier
RNLI Lifeboat Station
Tate Modern
Rose Theatre Exhibition
Vinoyolis
London Bridge Hospital
London Bridge City Pier
Thames Path
HMS Belfast
Southwark Cathedral
DUKE STREET HILL
Hay's Galleria
Southwark Crown Court
TOWER BRIDGE
The Scoop
Borough Market
LONDON BRIDGE STATION
The Shard
City Hall (London Assembly)
Kings College London
Guy's Hospital
ST THOMAS STREET
BERMONDSEY
CRUCIFIX LANE
DRUID STREET
London City Mission
Fashion & Textile Museum
Leathermarket Gardens
Tyers Gate
THE BOROUGH
Empire Square
Tabard Garden
Newington Gardens
Inner London Crown Court
Henrywood Hall
Purbrook Street
Grange Walk
GRANGE ROAD
South Bank University
NEW KENT ROAD
Searles Road
Munton Road
Victory Place
Henshaw Street
Chatham Street
Darwin Street
Mandela Way
OLD KENT ROAD
WALWORTH
P
Q
R

South Bank Quick Reference Guide

TOP 25 SIGHTS AND EXPERIENCES

Imperial War Museum (▷ 24)
The First World War galleries are a highlight in this museum that focuses on the social impact of warfare through film, painting and sound archives. The atrium has been redesigned by Foster + Partners and displays a number of large exhibits.

London Eye (▷ 30)
On a clear day you can see 40km (25 miles) from the top, across London and as far as Windsor Castle (▷ 79). With three and a half million people stepping on board every year to enjoy the bird's-eye views, it is Britain's most popular paid tourist attraction.

Tate Modern (▷ 54)
At the foot of the Millennium Bridge and presenting a distinctive face to the Thames, Tate Modern welcomes nearly five million visitors each year. The building itself, a converted power station, is almost as fascinating as the art.

MORE TO SEE 64

Borough Market
City Hall
Golden Hinde II
Hayward Gallery
HMS *Belfast*
SEA LIFE London Aquarium
The Shard
Southwark Cathedral

ENTERTAINMENT 128

Clubs
Ministry of Sound
Film
BFI IMAX
BFI Southbank
Opera, Ballet and Concerts
Purcell Room
Queen Elizabeth Hall
Royal Festival Hall
Theaters
National Theatre
Old Vic
Shakespeare's Globe
Young Vic

EAT 140

British and Modern
Oxo Tower Bar, Brasserie and Restaurant
European
Baltic
Gastropubs/Bars
The Anchor
Anchor & Hope
Lighter Bites
Tate Modern Café

Waterloo Bridge and Thames River Walkway

Fleet Street to the Tower

On this tour, see where the Romans founded Londinium in the first century AD and discover the city's long and fascinating history through its architecture, from Sir Christopher Wren's magnificent churches to the great Tower of London, with stories to capture everyone's imagination.

Morning
Arrive early at **St. Paul's Cathedral** (right, ▷ 44–45) before the crowds descend to appreciate fully its magnificence. The cathedral opens for sightseeing at 8.30am, but there are services, usually at 7.30am and 8am, which you could attend. The branch of the pâtisserie **Paul** in Paternoster Square is the perfect place for to stop for a snack.

Mid-morning
Walk up St. Martin's Aldersgate to the **Museum of London** (left, ▷ 32–33) and spend some time exploring its excellent collection. Retracing your steps, turn left into Gresham Street. Ahead is **St. Lawrence Jewry Church**, with dark wooden pews and a gold-encrusted ceiling lit by chandeliers. Cross the Guildhall Square to visit the **Guildhall Art Gallery** (▷ 70).

Lunch
Walk down King Street and turn right into Cheapside for an early lunch at **The Café Below** (▷ 145) in the crypt of **St. Mary-le-Bow**, a Wren church with striking modern stained-glass windows. A statue of Captain John Smith (1580–1631), leader of the Virginia Colony at Jamestown, presides over the square.

After lunch, turn down Bow Churchyard passage, then turn right into Bow Lane, lined with smart shops and eateries, to cross Watling Street. On the left is the **Guild Church of St. Mary Aldermary,** last rebuilt by Wren in a Gothic style. It's worth stepping inside to admire the magnificent ceiling.

The ruins of the **Temple of Mithras** (▷ 75) stand amid the soaring glass-and-steel modernity of the City's financial institutions. Ahead you'll see the distinctive **30 St. Mary Axe** (▷ 66), known as "The Gherkin." Passing the great pillars of the **Mansion House**, with the Bank of England in view, do some window-shopping in the **Royal Exchange** (right, ▷ 126) before exploring the food stands in **Leadenhall Market** (▷ 71, 125).

Afternoon

Head down Philpot Lane to the Thames, pausing to admire Wren's towering **Monument** (to the Great Fire of London) on your right. The riverside Customs House Walkway will lead you to the **Tower of London** (below, ▷ 58–59). Aim to arrive by 2pm. Ideally you will have pre-booked your entrance ticket to avoid any waiting around. First, take a tour with one of the Yeoman Warders, then spend the rest of the afternoon soaking up the history.

Evening

Sit by the Thames and enjoy the views of Tower Bridge and the south bank of the river. Walk through to **St. Katharine Docks** (▷ 73) and stroll among the smart yachts in the marina. The renovated warehouses there house a host of bars and restaurants in which to relax. Alternatively, take the Circle Line from Tower Hill to Farringdon for a gastropub experience at **The Peasant** (▷ 150).

CLERKENWELL
ST LUKE'S
The City University
City University
Finsbury Leisure Centre
Ironmonger Row Baths
St John's Gate
St Bartholomew's Medical School
Charterhouse
Exhibition Halls
City University Business School
The Barbican
Guildhall School of Music & Drama
BARBICAN STATION
FARRINGDON STATION
Central London Markets (Smithfield)
St Bartholomew's the Great
Museum of London
HOLBORN CIRCUS
St Bartholomew's Hospital
CITY THAMESLINK STATION
NEWGATE STREET
Old Bailey (Central Criminal Court)
London Stock Exchange
Guildhall
Public Record Office
Dr Johnson's House
LUDGATE CIRCUS
St Paul's Cathedral
One New Change Shopping Centre
St Mary-le-Bow Church
Temple Church
St Bridewell Church
College of Arms
St Mary Aldermary Church
Inner Temple
Middle Temple
QUEEN VICTORIA STREET
BLACKFRIARS STATION
City of London School
Vintners' Hall
HMS President
Blackfriars Millennium Pier
Blackfriars Pier
Millennium Bridge
SOUTHWARK BRIDGE
Thames
Panorama Pier
Bankside Pier
Bankside Gallery
Shakespeare's Globe
Purdy Hicks Gallery
Tate Modern
Financial Times
The London Television Centre
Oxo Tower
Rose Theatre Exhibition
Vinopolis
Kings College London
London Nautical School
Lambeth Bridge
Kew Bridge
Hampton Court Bridge
Hampton Court Bridge
Kew Bridge
Lambeth Bridge
Millennium Bridge
Blackfriars Bridge

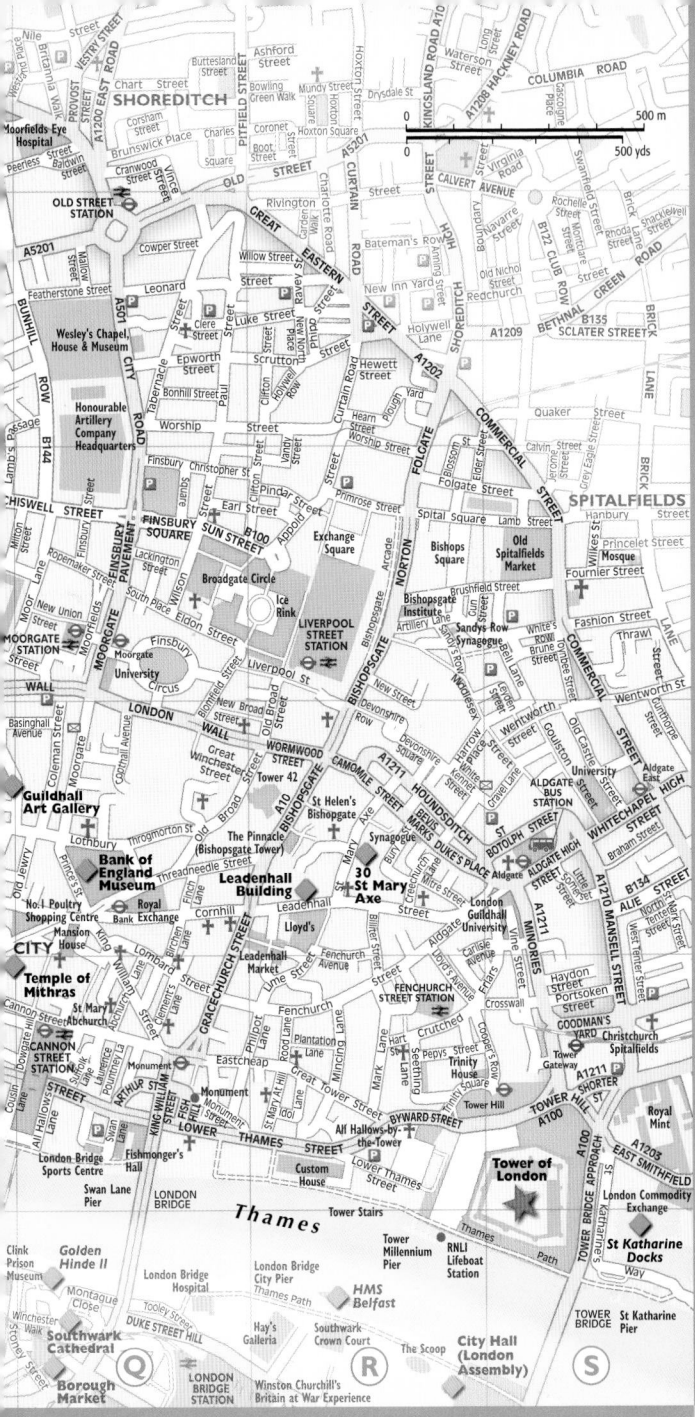
SHOREDITCH
Moorfields Eye Hospital
OLD STREET STATION
Wesley's Chapel House & Museum
Honourable Artillery Company Headquarters
FINSBURY SQUARE
Broadgate Circle
Ice Rink
LIVERPOOL STREET STATION
Exchange Square
Bishopsgate Institute
Sandys Row Synagogue
Bishops Square
Old Spitalfields Market
SPITALFIELDS
Princelet Street Mosque
MOORGATE STATION
Moorgate University
Guildhall Art Gallery
Tower 42
The Pinnacle (Bishopsgate Tower)
St Helen's Bishopsgate
Synagogue
ALDGATE BUS STATION
Bank of England Museum
Leadenhall Building
30 St Mary Axe
Royal Exchange
No.1 Poultry Shopping Centre
Lloyd's
London Guildhall University
Mansion House
CITY
Temple of Mithras
Leadenhall Market
FENCHURCH STREET STATION
Haydon Street
Portsoken Street
GOODMAN'S YARD
Christchurch Spitalfields
CANNON STREET STATION
Monument
Trinity House
Tower Gateway
Tower Hill
Royal Mint
All Hallows-by-the-Tower
London Bridge Sports Centre
Fishmonger's Hall
Custom House
Tower of London
Swan Lane Pier
LONDON BRIDGE
Tower Stairs
Thames
London Commodity Exchange
St Katharine Docks
Clink Prison Museum
Golden Hinde II
London Bridge Hospital
London Bridge City Pier
HMS Belfast
Tower Millennium Pier
RNLI Lifeboat Station
Southwark Cathedral
Hay's Galleria
Southwark Crown Court
City Hall (London Assembly)
Borough Market
LONDON BRIDGE STATION
Winston Churchill's Britain at War Experience
TOWER BRIDGE
St Katharine Pier
Q
R
S
0
500 m
0
500 yds

Fleet Street to the Tower
Quick Reference Guide

TOP 25 SIGHTS AND EXPERIENCES

Museum of London (▷ 32)
There is no better place to get an overview of the city's history, from prehistoric times to the present day, than at this museum. Its fascinating exhibits are so well displayed, it would be hard not to be engrossed. The museum even stands where the city first began, on the site of the Roman fort.

St. Paul's Cathedral (▷ 44)
Five monarchs oversaw the building of Sir Christopher Wren's masterpiece, completed in 1710, and ever since it has been the place where events of national importance are celebrated, mourned and commemorated. Come in the early evening, to listen to the choir sing evensong.

Tower of London (▷ 58)
As it is one of London's most popular sights, it's definitely worth pre-booking your entry tickets for the Tower, especially during the high-season summer months. A tour with a Yeoman Warder (known as a Beefeater) as your guide is an experience that you'll always remember.

MORE TO SEE 64

30 St. Mary Axe
Bank of England Museum
Guildhall Art Gallery
St. Bartholomew-the-Great
St. Katharine Docks
Temple Church
Temple of Mithras

SHOP 118

Street Markets
Leadenhall Market
Petticoat Lane
Spitalfields Market

ENTERTAINMENT 128

Clubs
Fabric
Events
Broadgate Centre
Opera, Ballet and Concerts
Barbican Concert Hall
Theaters
Barbican Centre Theatre

EAT 140

Asian
Banh Mi Bay
British and Modern
The Café Below
Medcalf
Restaurant at St Paul's
St. John
European
Bevis Marks Restaurant
Club Gascon
Famous Chefs
Fifteen
Gastropubs/Bars
The Peasant

A Routemaster bus outside St. Paul's

Covent Garden to Regent's Park

Literary associations, museums great and quirky, fine art and fun shopping all combine on this walk, which takes in busy streets and quiet corners. Here you'll find Theatreland, the heart of London's entertainment industry, lively Chinatown and Soho.

Morning

From Holborn Underground station, turn off Kingsway to enter Lincoln's Inn Fields. On its northern side, **Sir John Soane's Museum** (left, ▷ 74) is wonderfully atmospheric. As you cross the leafy square, look to the left to see the impressive brick buildings of Lincoln's Inn, one of the Inns of Court. With its outdoor terraces and open kitchen, **Fields Bar & Kitchen**, at the heart of Lincoln's Inn Fields, may tempt you to a coffee or something more substantial, before continuing on to **The Old Curiosity Shop**, built in 1567, immortalized by Charles Dickens and now displaying handmade shoes. Following St. Clement's Lane will take you through the London School of Economics' campus and out alongside the Royal Courts of Justice to the Strand, where Wren's **St. Clement Danes Church** sits on an island amid busy traffic.

Mid-morning

Continue west along the Strand to **Somerset House** (▷ 50–51) to admire the great courtyard and immerse yourself in French Impressionist art at the **Courtauld Gallery** (below, ▷ 51).

Lunch
Eat lunch in grand surroundings in Somerset House or walk up Wellington Street into lively **Covent Garden**, which is packed with cafés, restaurants and bars. **Joe Allen** (▷ 148) is a favourite. Turn left for the **Piazza** (▷ 69). Here you can shop and enjoy the buzz in the former market (right). Cross Long Acre for the trendy shops on Neal Street.

Afternoon
Passing the brightly coloured high-rise blocks on St. Giles High Street, visit **St. Giles-in-the-Fields**, a handsome church with a Palladian interior, founded by Queen Matilda in 1101 as a leper hospital. Continue down Denmark Street, famed for its music connections, and cross Charing Cross Road with Foyles, London's most famous bookshop, on the left, to reach leafy **Soho Square**. In the 17th century, this was one of the most fashionable places to live. Today the area is home to the film and recording industries and numerous pubs and restaurants.

Mid-afternoon
Leave at Frith Street, go right at the **Dog and Duck** pub (▷ 146), and stop for refreshment as you zigzag your way through cobbled Meard Street and across Wardour Street to the lively fruit and textiles **market** on Berwick Street. A left turn on Broadwick Street and another left down Lexington Street will take you among the specialist shops of Brewer Street and back onto Wardour Street. Cross Shaftesbury Avenue and turn left into Gerrard Street, the start of **Chinatown**.

Evening
Stroll through **Chinatown** (right) and pick a restaurant that takes your fancy. Shaftesbury Avenue is the heart of **Theatreland**, **Piccadilly Circus** is a short walk away and **Soho** buzzes with restaurants and nightlife.

Regent's Park
REGENT'S PARK
St John's Lodge
Open Air Theatre
Queen Mary's Garden
Regent's College
Madame Tussaud's
University of Westminster
Royal Academy of Music
Royal College of Physicians
Royal National Orthopaedic Hospital
Great Portland Street
Euston Tower
EUSTON STATION
University College Hospital
BT Tower
University of Westminster
UCL
Central Synagogue
MARYLEBONE
Wallace Collection
Wigmore Hall
All Saints' Church
Selfridges'
Photographers' Gallery
Handel House Museum
St George's Church
US Embassy
Roosevelt Memorial
Church of the Immaculate Conception
MAYFAIR
Royal Academy of Arts
St James's Church
Spencer House
Marlborough House
0
500 m
0
500 yds
1
2
3
4
5
6
F
G
H

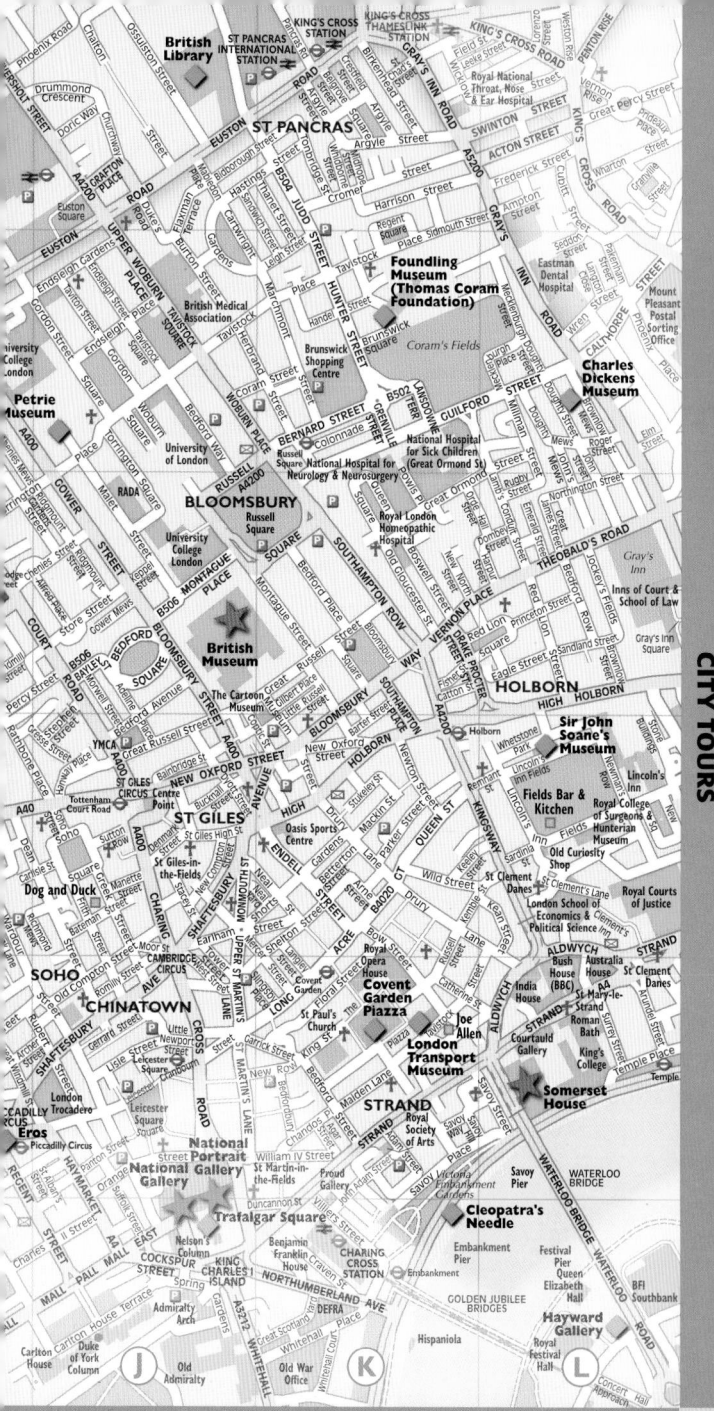
British Library
ST PANCRAS INTERNATIONAL STATION
KING'S CROSS STATION
KING'S CROSS THAMESLINK STATION
ST PANCRAS
Foundling Museum (Thomas Coram Foundation)
Coram's Fields
Brunswick Shopping Centre
British Medical Association
Petrie Museum
University of London
National Hospital for Neurology & Neurosurgery
National Hospital for Sick Children (Great Ormond St)
Charles Dickens Museum
BLOOMSBURY
Russell Square
University College London
Royal London Homeopathic Hospital
British Museum
The Cartoon Museum
HOLBORN
Sir John Soane's Museum
Inns of Court & School of Law
Gray's Inn
Gray's Inn Square
Fields Bar & Kitchen
Royal College of Surgeons & Hunterian Museum
Lincoln's Inn
Old Curiosity Shop
ST GILES
St Giles-in-the-Fields
Oasis Sports Centre
Dog and Duck
St Clement Danes
London School of Economics & Political Science
Royal Courts of Justice
SOHO
CHINATOWN
Covent Garden Piazza
Royal Opera House
St Paul's Church
Joe Allen
London Transport Museum
India House
Australia House
St Mary-le-Strand
Roman Bath
Courtauld Gallery
King's College
Somerset House
STRAND
Royal Society of Arts
Eros
Piccadilly Circus
London Trocadero
National Portrait Gallery
Trafalgar Square
Cleopatra's Needle
Savoy Pier
WATERLOO BRIDGE
Embankment Pier
Festival Pier
Queen Elizabeth Hall
BFI Southbank
Hayward Gallery
Royal Festival Hall
GOLDEN JUBILEE BRIDGES
Hispaniola
Admiralty Arch
Nelson's Column
Benjamin Franklin House
CHARING CROSS STATION
Embankment
Carlton House Terrace
Duke of York Column
Old Admiralty
Old War Office
J
K
L

Covent Garden to Regent's Park
Quick Reference Guide

SIGHTS AND EXPERIENCES

British Museum (▷ 16)
This is one of the world's greatest museums, where you can travel the globe through exhibits from every civilization, spanning over two million years of human history. World-famous objects include the Rosetta Stone, Parthenon sculptures and Egyptian mummies. With eight million artifacts in the collection, excellent special exhibitions, events, talks and activities, you may find you visit more than once.

Somerset House (▷ 50)
In summer, fountains play in the courtyard; in winter it becomes an outdoor ice rink. Whenever you visit, there's likely to be something happening, from contemporary art and design exhibitions to open air concerts and films. Twice a year it hosts London Fashion Week. Spanning Old Masters and Impressionist masterpieces, the art collection at the Courtauld Gallery is superb.

MORE TO SEE 64

British Library
Charles Dickens Museum
Cleopatra's Needle
Covent Garden Piazza
Eros
Foundling Museum
Handel House Museum
London Transport Museum
Madame Tussaud's
Petrie Museum
Photographers' Gallery
Regent's Park and ZSL London Zoo
Sir John's Soane Museum
Wallace Collection

SHOP 118

Art and Antiques
Grays Antiques Market
Books
Stanfords
Department Stores
Liberty
Selfridges
Fashion
Brora
Browns
Burberry Beauty Box
Food and Drink
Rococo
Villandry
Health and Beauty
Neal's Yard Remedies
Homeware
Aram Designs Ltd
Heal's
Designers Guild
Thomas Goode Ltd
Toys
Benjamin Pollock's Toyshop
Hamleys

ENTERTAINMENT 128

Clubs
The Borderline
Guanabara
Salsa!
Jazz
Jazz After Dark
Pizza Express Jazz Club Soho
Opera, Ballet and Concerts
London Coliseum
Royal Opera House
Wigmore Hall
Theaters
Donmar Warehouse
Theatre Royal, Drury Lane

EAT 140

Asian
Benares
Chaopraya Eat-Thai
Masala Zone
Rasa W1
Brasseries/Brunch
Christopher's
Joe Allen
British and Modern
Rules
European
Gaby's Deli
Hibiscus
Icebar London
Villandry
Wild Honey
Famous Chefs
The Square
Tom's Kitchen
Gastropubs/Bars
Grand Café
Lowlander
Lighter Bites
Paul
Vegetarian
Food for Thought
Wild Food Café

Westminster and St. James's

Westminster Abbey, the Houses of Parliament, Buckingham Palace, Trafalgar Square—some of London's most famous landmarks are located in Westminster. Follow in the footsteps of royalty as you take in famous art galleries, London's prettiest royal park and some upscale shopping.

Morning
Begin your day at **Trafalgar Square** (▷ 75), where Sir Edwin Landseer's lions proudly protect Nelson's Column. Presiding over its northern side, the **National Gallery** (▷ 34–35) shows Western European art in a stately setting. Next door, the **National Portrait Gallery** (above, ▷ 36–37) puts faces to famous names down the centuries. Both galleries have good cafés, but you may also like the nearby **Café in the Crypt** at **St. Martin-in-the-Fields** (▷ 138). Perhaps book for a candlelit concert while you are there.

Mid-morning
Walk down Whitehall to visit the **Banqueting House** (right, ▷ 14–15), noted for its Rubens ceiling, and to see the colorful **Horse Guards** and the **Cenotaph** war memorial. You soon arrive at **Big Ben** and the **Houses of Parliament** (▷ 22–23). There are splendid views of the River Thames from Westminster Bridge, immortalized by poet William Wordsworth and Impressionist Claude Monet. **Westminster Abbey** (▷ 62–63) lies across the square.

Lunch
Turn up Storey's Gate to **St. James's Park** (▷ 42–43), perhaps picking up a sandwich en route to eat in this pretty royal park. Alternatively, try **Inn the Park** (▷ 148). You will pass the **Churchill War Rooms** (▷ 67) beneath a sweeping flight of steps, watched over by the statue of an imperious Clive of India, and may wish to return there after lunch. Stroll among the park's trees and flowerbeds and watch the ducks, geese and pelicans feeding on the lake.

Afternoon
Crossing the Mall, a wide ceremonial route packed with crowds on great occasions, you will see **Buckingham Palace** (above, ▷ 18–19) on your left, fronted by the Queen Victoria Memorial. Walk up the Mall to get a closer look at the palace, or cross to Marlborough Road alongside the red-brick **St. James's Palace.** A working royal palace, setting for official receptions, it houses the Household Office of Prince William and Prince Harry. **Clarence House** (▷ 68), home of Prince Charles and the Duchess of Cornwall, is on the far side of the palace.

Mid-afternoon
St. James's Street is lined with old-established businesses and famously exclusive members' clubs. Turn right into Jermyn Street for more quintessentially British shops, many carrying the Royal Warrant. Walking through the elegant Piccadilly Arcade brings you into Piccadilly, where **Fortnum & Mason** (▷ 124) is the perfect place for afternoon tea. **Hatchards** (▷ 125), booksellers since 1797, is next door. Visit **St. James's, Piccadilly** (▷ 73), Wren's church for the local aristocracy. There may be a concert on there in the evening.

Evening
If you like the Grand Café tradition, **The Wolseley** (▷ 151) is for you. Or dress up for a meal at **Greenhouse** (▷ 147) in Mayfair. Alternatively, reserve an evening Thames River **dinner cruise** (left, ▷ 56–57).

MAYFAIR
Church of the Immaculate Conception
Greenhouse (Hay's Mews)
Royal Academy of Arts
St James's Church
Hatchards
Fortnum & Mason
PICCADILLY
The Wolseley
Green Park
Spencer House
Marlborough House
Queen Alexandra Memorial
St James's Palace
Queen Chapel
Clarence House
Lancaster House
Green Park
Apsley House
Wellington Arch
HYDE PARK CORNER
PARK LANE
DUKE OF WELLINGTON PLACE
Constitution Hill
Buckingham Palace
Queen Victoria Memorial
Buckingham Palace Gardens
Queen's Gallery
Royal Mews
Wellington Barracks
BUCKINGHAM GATE
LOWER GROSVENOR PLACE
GROSVENOR PLACE
BELGRAVE PLACE
KING'S ROAD
EATON SQUARE
ECCLESTON PLACE
Cardinal Place Shopping Centre
Westminster City School
Westminster City Hall
VICTORIA STREET
Westminster Cathedral
VICTORIA BUS STATION
VICTORIA STATION
Victoria Place Shopping Centre
The Colonnades Shopping Centre
VICTORIA COACH STATION
Queen Mother Sports Centre
VAUXHALL BRIDGE
ROCHESTER WAY
BELGRAVE ROAD
WARWICK
500 m
500 yds
F
G
H

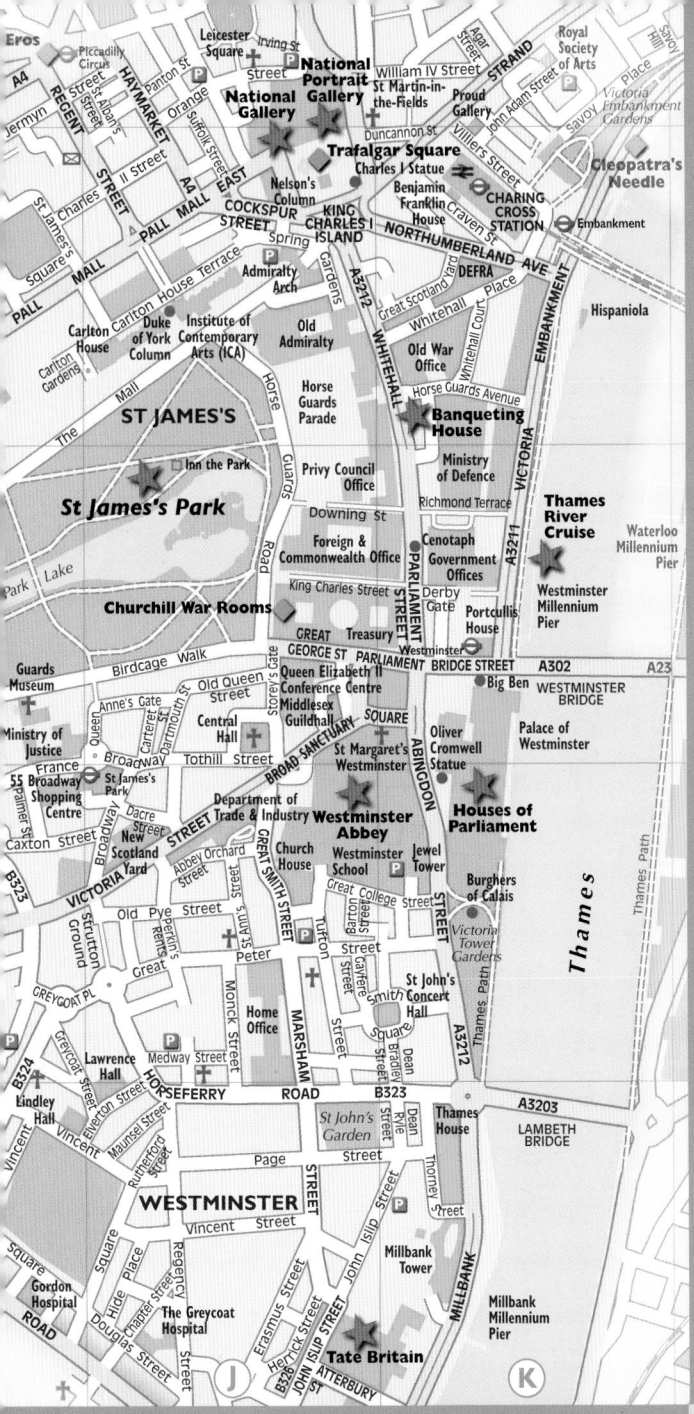
Eros
Piccadilly Circus
Leicester Square
Irving St
National Portrait Gallery
National Gallery
William IV Street
St Martin-in-the-Fields
Duncannon St
Proud Gallery
Adam Street
STRAND
Royal Society of Arts
John Adam Street
Savoy Place
Victoria Embankment Gardens
Villiers Street
Trafalgar Square
Charles I Statue
Cleopatra's Needle
Nelson's Column
Benjamin Franklin House
CHARING CROSS STATION
Embankment
Craven St
NORTHUMBERLAND AVE
KING CHARLES I ISLAND
COCKSPUR STREET
PALL MALL EAST
A4
REGENT STREET
HAYMARKET
Jermyn Street
Panton St
Orange Street
Suffolk Street
St Alban's Street
Charles II Street
St James's Square
PALL MALL
Spring Gardens
Admiralty Arch
A3212
Great Scotland Yard
Whitehall Place
DEFRA
Hispaniola
Carlton House Terrace
Carlton House
Duke of York Column
Institute of Contemporary Arts (ICA)
Old Admiralty
Old War Office
Whitehall Court
WHITEHALL
EMBANKMENT
Carlton Gardens
The Mall
Horse Guards Parade
Horse Guards Avenue
Banqueting House
ST JAMES'S
Inn the Park
Privy Council Office
Ministry of Defence
VICTORIA
St James's Park
Richmond Terrace
Thames River Cruise
Waterloo Millennium Pier
Park Lane
Lake
Foreign & Commonwealth Office
Cenotaph
Government Offices
A3211
Westminster Millennium Pier
Churchill War Rooms
King Charles Street
PARLIAMENT STREET
Derby Gate
Portcullis House
GREAT Treasury
Guards Museum
Birdcage Walk
GEORGE ST
Queen Elizabeth II Conference Centre
PARLIAMENT
Westminster
BRIDGE STREET
A302
A23
Big Ben
WESTMINSTER BRIDGE
Old Queen Street
Strutt's Gate
Anne's Gate
Carteret St
Dartmouth St
Queen
Central Hall
Middlesex Guildhall
SQUARE
Ministry of Justice
Broadway
Tothill Street
BROAD SANCTUARY
St Margaret's Westminster
ABINGDON
Oliver Cromwell Statue
Palace of Westminster
France
55 Broadway Shopping Centre
St James's Park
Palmer St
Department of Trade & Industry
Westminster Abbey
Houses of Parliament
Caxton Street
Dacre Street
STREET
New Scotland Yard
Broadway
Abbey Orchard Street
Church House
Westminster School
Jewel Tower
Great College Street
Burghers of Calais
B3323
VICTORIA
GREAT SMITH STREET
Old Pye Street
Strutton Ground
Tufton Street
Cayley Street
Victoria Tower Gardens
Thames
Thames Path
Great Peter Street
Smith Square
St John's Concert Hall
GREYCOAT PL
Monck Street
Home Office
MARSHAM
Dean Bradley Street
A3212
Lawrence Hall
Medway Street
B324
HORSEFERRY ROAD
B323
A3203
Lindley Hall
Elverton Street
Maunsel Street
St John's Garden
Dean Rye Street
Thames House
LAMBETH BRIDGE
Vincent
Rutherford Street
Page Street
WESTMINSTER
Thorney Street
Vincent Street
Millbank Tower
Square
Regency Place
Gordon Hospital
Hide Place
Chapter Street
The Greycoat Hospital
Douglas Street
Erasmus Street
Herrick Street
B3528
JOHN ISLIP STREET
ATTERBURY ST
Tate Britain
MILLBANK
Millbank Millennium Pier
J
K

Westminster and St. James's
Quick Reference Guide

TOP 25 SIGHTS AND EXPERIENCES

Banqueting House (▷ 14)
Inigo Jones's 17th-century architectural masterpiece has a magnificent Rubens ceiling.

Buckingham Palace (▷ 18)
The summer opening of this royal residence and office of the Royal Household is not to be missed.

Houses of Parliament (▷ 22)
Britain is governed from this landmark Victorian Gothic building on the banks of the Thames.

National Gallery (▷ 34)
The superb collection gives a overview of European painting from Giotto to Cézanne.

National Portrait Gallery (▷ 36)
The famous and the infamous, past and present, are portrayed in paintings and photographs.

St. James's Park (▷ 42)
Tree-filled, surrounded by palaces and with a lake at its heart, this is the prettiest of the royal parks.

Tate Britain (▷ 52)
Tate Britain exhibits British art from 1500 to the 21st century, with a whole gallery devoted to Turner.

Thames River Cruise (▷ 56)
Sit down, relax and enjoy views of some of the most beautiful and interesting buildings in London.

Westminster Abbey (▷ 62)
The vast abbey is full of exquisite detail and monuments. Herein lies a pageant of British history.

MORE TO SEE 64

Apsley House
Churchill War Rooms
Clarence House
Green Park
Royal Academy of Arts
St. James's, Piccadilly
Spencer House
Trafalgar Square

SHOP 118

Art and Antiques
Agnews
Books
Hatchards
Department Stores
Fortnum & Mason
Fashion
Turnbull & Asser

ENTERTAINMENT 128

Comedy
The Comedy Store
Concerts
St. James's, Piccadilly
St. Martin-in-the-Fields
Dancing
The Ritz
Film
Institute of Contemporary Arts (ICA)

EAT 140

Asian
Tamarind
British and Modern
Portrait Restaurant
The Wolseley
Famous Chefs
Le Gavroche
Greenhouse
International
Gaucho
Lighter Bites
Inn the Park

Around Hyde Park

A feast of world-class museums and music put South Kensington firmly on every visitor's must-see list. Adjoining Hyde Park, Kensington Gardens come complete with a romantic royal palace and memories of Diana, Princess of Wales, who lived there.

Morning
At **South Kensington Underground** station there's a passage marked "To the Museums." Follow it, or come up to street level for a fortifying breakfast at one of the many cafés and pâtisseries that crowd this popular area. You are heading for the Cromwell Road and three world-class museums: The **Victoria and Albert Museum** (left, ▷ 60–61), the **Natural History Museum** (▷ 38–39) and the **Science Museum** (▷ 46–47). They are free, so you could pop into each one to get an idea of their riches, or spend the morning engrossed in the subjects that interest you most.

Mid-morning
All three museums have **cafés** to retreat to for sustenance. The café at the V&A is located in what was the world's first museum restaurant, in rooms intended as a showpiece of modern design and craftsmanship. During summer you can eat outdoors. The cafés at the Science and Natural History museums are particularly child-friendly.

Lunch
Walk up Exhibition Road toward **Hyde Park** (▷ 71), turning left at Prince Consort Road to view the stately **Royal College of Music** and to approach the elliptical **Royal Albert Hall** (▷ 137). **Verdi, an Italian Kitchen** upstairs is a good lunch spot and you could perhaps make reservations for a concert or tour. Look at the detail on the frieze that rings this distinctive domed building and, going west, don't miss the reliefs and *sgraffito* that decorate the facade of the building opposite, previously occupied by the Royal College of Organists.

Afternoon
Cross Kensington Gore to the **Albert Memorial** (right, ▷ 66), an ornate fantasy in glittering gold by George Gilbert Scott. Stroll through **Kensington Gardens** (▷ 26–27) to the Diana, Princess of Wales Memorial Fountain in adjacent Hyde Park. Then take the path back through Kensington Gardens via the Round Pond to **Kensington Palace** (▷ 26–27).

Mid-afternoon
Tour Kensington Palace and take afternoon tea in **The Orangery** (▷ 149). Leaving by the Kensington Palace Gardens exit and "billionaires' row" of embassies, cross Kensington Church Street to the specialist shops and galleries along **Holland Street**. Turn left down **Kensington Church Walk** for exquisite little shops, courtyard houses and gardens. This is a secret, village-like London yet only seconds away from busy Kensington High Street.

Dinner
Babylon (▷ 144), with its rooftop gardens and fabulous views across London, is nearby, as is Kensington favorite **Maggie Jones's** (▷ 148). Or you could take the bus to Knightsbridge, go shopping and relax in the **Champagne Bar** at **Harrods** (below, ▷ 125).

Kensington Gardens
Round Pond
Kensington Palace
The Orangery
Peter Pan Statue
Speke's Monument
Physical Energy Statue
Serpentine Gallery
West Carriage Drive
Albert Memorial
Alexandra Gate
Portobello Road Market
Jubilee Walk
The Broad Walk
Palace Avenue
Kensington Palace Gardens
Kensington Market
KENSINGTON ROAD
HYDE PARK GATE
KENSINGTON GORE
Royal College of Art
Royal Albert Hall
Royal Geographical Society
Imperial College of Science
Prince Consort Road
Royal College of Music
Imperial College
Imperial College Road
Hyde Park Chapel
Science Museum
Earth Galleries
Natural History Museum
KENSINGTON
Cottesmore Gardens
Victoria Grove
Queen's Gate Terrace
Queen's Gate Place
Queen's Gate Place Mews
Queen's Gate Mews
Queen's Gate Gardens
Queen's Gate
Queen's Gate Mews
Queen's Gate Place
Queen's Gate Place Mews
Queen's Gate Gardens
Queen's Gate
Queen's Gate
Queen's Gate

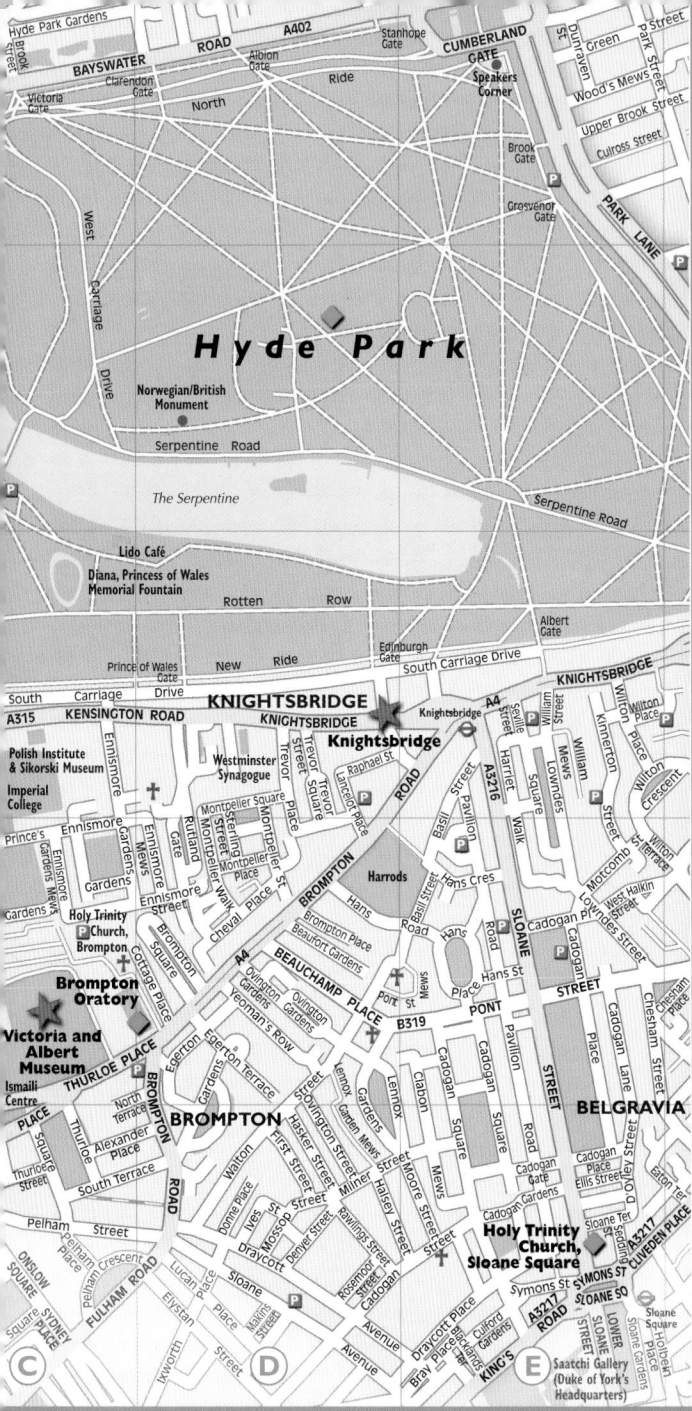
Hyde Park
The Serpentine
Serpentine Road
Norwegian/British Monument
Lido Café
Diana, Princess of Wales Memorial Fountain
Rotten Row
Hyde Park Gardens
Brook Street
BAYSWATER ROAD
A402
Albion Gate
Clarendon Gate
Victoria Gate
North Ride
Stanhope Gate
CUMBERLAND GATE
Speakers Corner
Dunraven St
Green Street
Park Street
Wood's Mews
Upper Brook Street
Culross Street
Brook Gate
Grosvenor Gate
PARK LANE
West Carriage Drive
Albert Gate
Edinburgh Gate
Prince of Wales Gate
New Ride
South Carriage Drive
South Carriage Drive
KNIGHTSBRIDGE
A315
KENSINGTON ROAD
KNIGHTSBRIDGE
Knightsbridge
A4
Knightsbridge
Polish Institute & Sikorski Museum
Imperial College
Westminster Synagogue
Raphael St
Trevor Square
Trevor Place
Lancelot Place
Montpelier Square
Montpelier Street
Montpelier Place
Montpelier Walk
Rutland Gardens
Ennismore Gardens
Ennismore Mews
Ennismore Street
Prince's Gardens
Holy Trinity Church, Brompton
Cheval Place
BROMPTON ROAD
Harrods
Basil Street
Pavilion Road
A3216
Harriet Walk
Lowndes Square
Lowndes Street
William Mews
Wilton Place
Wilton Crescent
Wilton Terrace
Kinnerton Street
Motcomb Street
West Halkin Street
Hans Cres
Hans Place
Hans Road
Brompton Place
Beaufort Gardens
SLOANE STREET
Cadogan Place
Cadogan Gate
Cadogan Lane
Chesham Place
Chesham Street
Brompton Square
Cottage Place
Brompton Oratory
A4
BEAUCHAMP PLACE
Pont St
Pont Mews
Pont Street
Yeoman's Row
Ovington Gardens
Ovington Square
B319
Victoria and Albert Museum
Ismaili Centre
THURLOE PLACE
Thurloe Place
Thurloe Street
Alexander Place
South Terrace
Pelham Street
Pelham Crescent
FULHAM ROAD
Edgeworth Terrace
Edgeworth Gardens
BROMPTON
BROMPTON ROAD
Walton Street
Jonathan Street
Lennox Gardens
Lennox Gardens Mews
Cadogan Square
Cadogan Square
Cadogan Place
Ellis Street
Sloane Ter
Sloane Square
Holy Trinity Church, Sloane Square
BELGRAVIA
A3217
CLIVEDEN PLACE
SYMONS ST
SLOANE SQ
LOWER SLOANE STREET
Sloane Square
Hobart Place
Sloane Gardens
Symons St
Draycott Place
Draycott Avenue
Bray Place
Milner Street
Moore Street
Halsey Street
Rawlings Street
Rosemoor Street
Cadogan Place
Cadogan Gardens
Clifford Gardens
KING'S
Sloane Avenue
Elystan Place
Ixworth Place
Makins Street
SIDNEY SQUARE
ONSLOW SQUARE
Saatchi Gallery (Duke of York's Headquarters)
C
D
E

Around Hyde Park
Quick Reference Guide

TOP 25 SIGHTS AND EXPERIENCES

Kensington Palace and Gardens (▷ 26)
This historic royal palace, set in the 110ha (275-acre) Kensington Gardens, was home to Queen Victoria and more recently Diana, Princess of Wales.

Knightsbridge Shopping (▷ 28)
Knightsbridge's shops enthral the most dedicated fashionista, with window displays to delight the eye. Don't miss those famous London landmarks: Harvey Nichols and Harrods.

Natural History Museum (▷ 38)
With everything that you have ever wanted to know about the natural world and a whole lot more under one roof, the museum is a truly fascinating place.

Science Museum (▷ 46)
With exhibits ranging from Stephenson's steam locomotive *Rocket* to a space capsule, and with an IMAX cinema and plenty of hands-on fun, the museum makes science entertaining.

Victoria and Albert Museum (▷ 60)
This wonderful treasure house of decorative arts, one of the largest collections of its kind in the world, delights, inspires and often surprises.

MORE TO SEE 64

Albert Memorial
Brompton Oratory
Holy Trinity, Sloane Square
Hyde Park
Peter Pan Statue

SHOP 118

Art and Antiques
Kensington Church Street
Department Stores
Harrods
Harvey Nichols
Peter Jones
Fashion
Jimmy Choo
Lulu Guinness

ENTERTAINMENT 128

Film
Ciné Lumière
Opera, Ballet and Concerts
Cadogan Hall
Holland Park Theatre
Royal Albert Hall
Theaters
Royal Court/Jerwood Theatre Upstairs

EAT 140

Asian
Amaya
Royal China
British and Modern
Babylon
Bibendum
Maggie Jones's
Famous Chefs
Maze
Lighter Bites
The Orangery

Farther Afield

Birthplace of Henry VIII and Elizabeth I, home to the National Maritime Museum and famed for the Royal Observatory, Greenwich (▷ 20–21) makes a great escape from central London, with open parkland, river views and a lively market selling food and crafts.

Morning

The perfect way to travel to Greenwich is by boat, as the royals did in centuries past, for the **Old Royal Naval College** (above, ▷ 20) presents a splendid baroque facade to the river. Alternatively, the Docklands Light Railway (DLR) gets you there quickly. Make your first stop the **Discover Greenwich** tourist information center, which has an excellent exhibition on the **Maritime Greenwich World Heritage Site** and the very good **Old Brewery** café/bar (tel 020 3327 1280). Located in the Pepys Building, it is close to the magnificent ***Cutty Sark***, the world's last tea clipper, restored after serious fire damage.

Mid-morning

Cross Romney Road to visit the **National Maritime Museum** (right, ▷ 21) and delve into all matters nautical, with plenty of hands-on exhibits. A colonnade links the museum with the elegant Palladian-style **Queen's House**, designed by Inigo Jones in the 17th-century. Today it houses a fine art collection with works by Gainsborough, Reynolds and Turner. Back across Romney Road, visit the neo-classical **Chapel of St. Peter and St. Paul** and the magnificent **Painted Hall** of the Old Royal Naval College. The ceiling here took 19 years to complete and the artist, James Thornhill, was eventually knighted for his labors. It was here that the body of Admiral Lord Nelson lay in state after the Battle of Trafalgar.

Lunch
There's a good **restaurant** downstairs in the Old Royal Naval College, or for something less formal you could choose to return to the **Old Brewery** in the Pepys Building.

Afternoon
Now head up the hill in Greenwich Park to the **Royal Observatory** (above, ▷ 21), commissioned by Charles II and designed by Wren in 1675 with the purpose of finding longitude at sea. The Time galleries' exhibits, interactive **Astronomy Centre** and the **Peter Harrison Planetarium** are fascinating. Here you can stand astride the **Greenwich Meridian** line.

Mid-afternoon
Covering 74ha (183 acres) **Greenwich Park** is the oldest enclosed royal park, with rose gardens, a flower garden, lake, wilderness deer park and fine views across the Thames to Docklands and the City of London (left). Follow a path leading to Regency houses on Crooms Hill and continue downhill to the lively weekend **market**, packed with food stalls, crafts and small design shops.

Dinner
Take the DLR to **Canary Wharf** (▷ 76), in the heart of Docklands, to eat at the 18th-century waterside pub **The Gun** (▷ 147), once the haunt of smugglers and Lord Nelson's favorite trysting place.

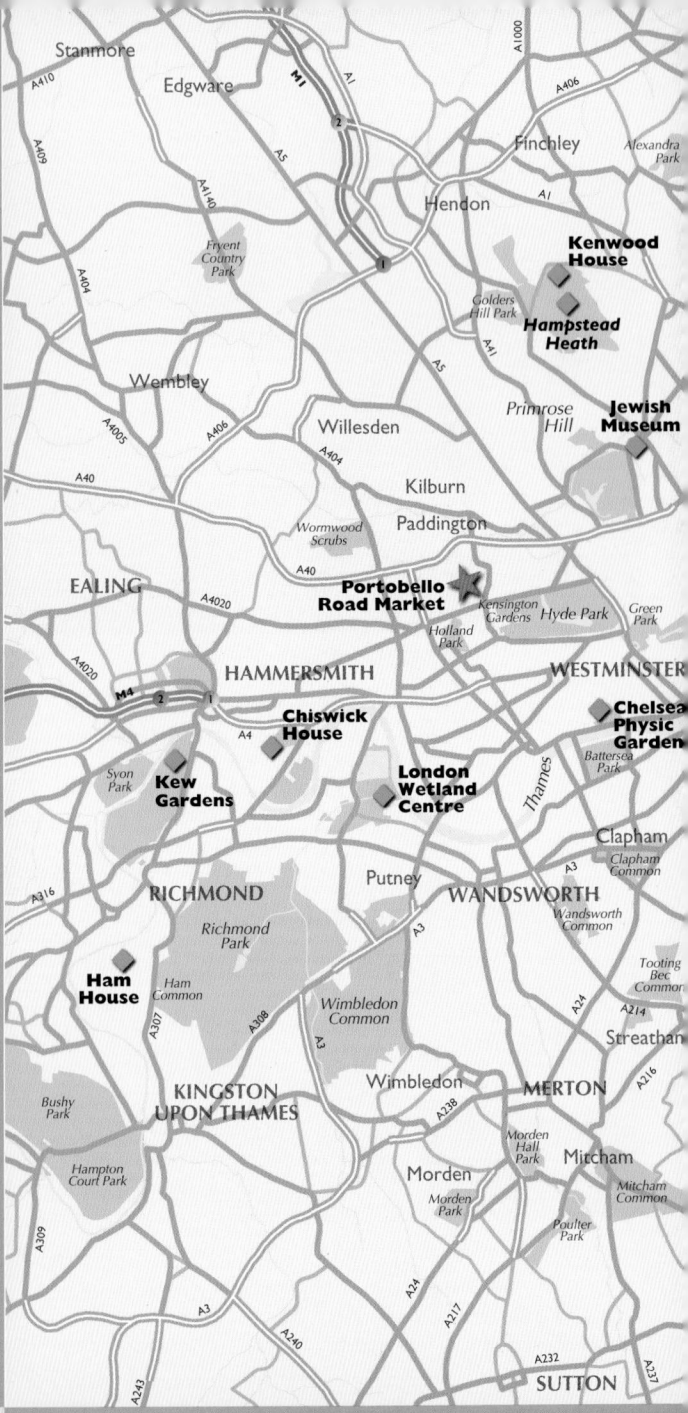
Stanmore
Edgware
M1
A1
A1000
A406
A410
A409
A5
A4140
Finchley
Alexandra Park
Hendon
A1
Kenwood House
Fryent Country Park
A404
Golders Hill Park
Hampstead Heath
A41
A5
Wembley
Primrose Hill
Jewish Museum
A4005
A406
Willesden
A404
A40
Kilburn
Wormwood Scrubs
Paddington
A40
EALING
Portobello Road Market
A4020
Kensington Gardens
Hyde Park
Green Park
Holland Park
A4020
HAMMERSMITH
WESTMINSTER
M4
A4
Chiswick House
Chelsea Physic Garden
Battersea Park
Syon Park
Kew Gardens
London Wetland Centre
Thames
Clapham
Clapham Common
A3
A316
RICHMOND
Putney
WANDSWORTH
Richmond Park
Wandsworth Common
A3
Ham House
Ham Common
Tooting Bec Common
A307
A308
Wimbledon Common
A24
A214
Streatham
A3
Wimbledon
MERTON
A216
Bushy Park
KINGSTON UPON THAMES
A238
Morden Hall Park
Mitcham
Hampton Court Park
Morden
Mitcham Common
Morden Park
Poulter Park
A309
A24
A3
A217
A240
A232
A337
A243
SUTTON

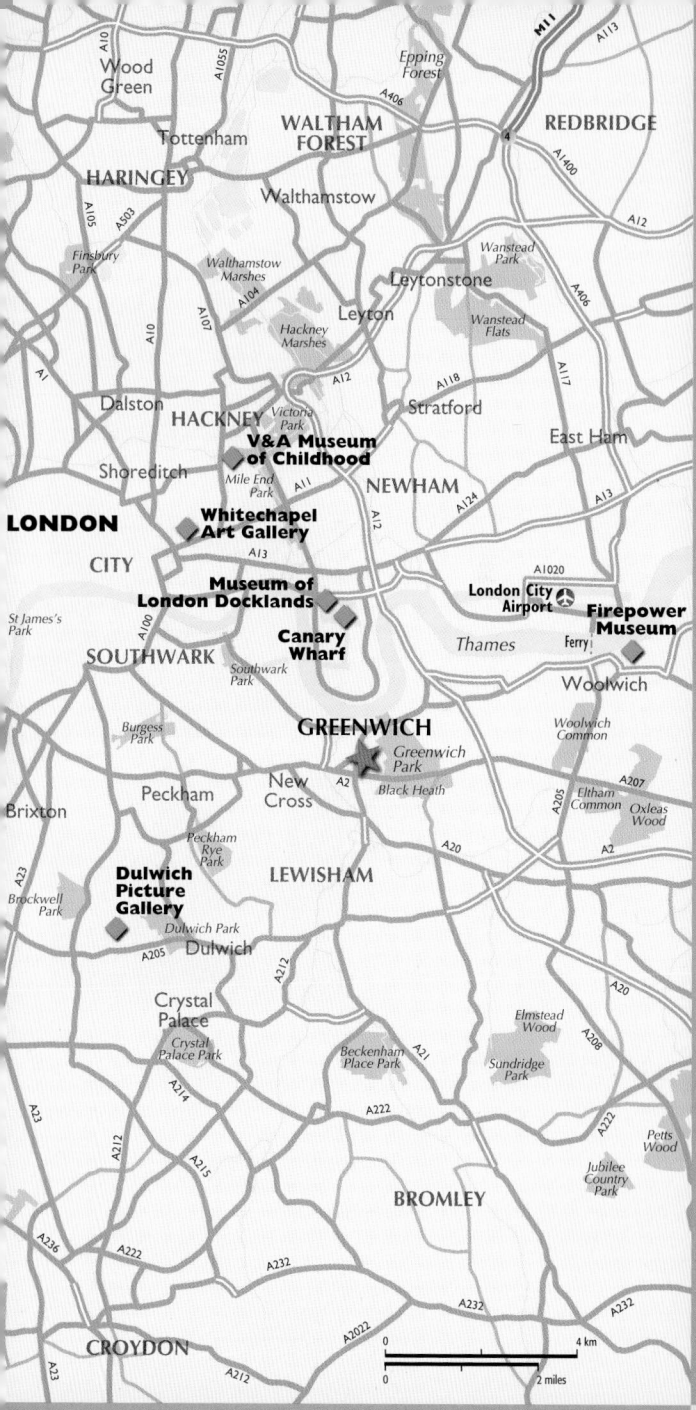
Wood Green
Tottenham
WALTHAM FOREST
REDBRIDGE
Epping Forest
HARINGEY
Walthamstow
Finsbury Park
Walthamstow Marshes
Wanstead Park
Leytonstone
Leyton
Hackney Marshes
Wanstead Flats
Dalston
HACKNEY
Victoria Park
Stratford
V&A Museum of Childhood
East Ham
Shoreditch
Mile End Park
NEWHAM
LONDON
Whitechapel Art Gallery
CITY
Museum of London Docklands
London City Airport
Firepower Museum
St James's Park
Canary Wharf
Thames
Ferry
SOUTHWARK
Southwark Park
Woolwich
Burgess Park
GREENWICH
Woolwich Common
Greenwich Park
Black Heath
Peckham
New Cross
Brixton
Eltham Common
Oxleas Wood
Peckham Rye Park
LEWISHAM
Dulwich Picture Gallery
Brockwell Park
Dulwich Park
Dulwich
Crystal Palace
Crystal Palace Park
Elmstead Wood
Beckenham Place Park
Sundridge Park
Petts Wood
Jubilee Country Park
BROMLEY
CROYDON
0
4 km
0
2 miles

Farther Afield Quick Reference Guide

TOP 25 SIGHTS AND EXPERIENCES

Greenwich (▷ 20)
The ideal way to spend a Sunday is to take a cruise on the Thames to Greenwich, a UNESCO World Heritage Site. Visit the great maritime sights and the Royal Observatory, take a leisurely stroll in historic Greenwich Park and shop in the lively crafts market.

Portobello Road Market (▷ 40)
Dedicate a Saturday to exploring the shops and stalls of an antiques market like no other. Whatever you're looking for, be it glass, china, curios or jewelry, it's likely you'll find it here, and searching for treasure and bargaining with the dealers is all part of the fun.

Kew Gardens (▷ 77)
An abundance of flowers, trees, plants and shrubs from around the globe grow in fantastic swathes across the landscapes and fill giant glasshouses in the world's most famous botanical garden. Take the treetop walkway for a bird's-eye view of the gardens.

MORE TO SEE 64

Canary Wharf
Chelsea Physic Garden
Chiswick House
Dulwich Picture Gallery
Firepower Museum
Ham House
Hampstead Heath
Jewish Museum
Kenwood House
London Wetland Centre
Museum of London Docklands
V&A Museum of Childhood
Whitechapel Art Gallery

SHOP 118

Books
Books for Cooks
Fashion
Start London
Shopping Centers
Westfield London
Street Markets
Bermondsey Antiques Market
Camden Markets

ENTERTAINMENT 128

Clubs
606 Club
Barfly
Bush Hall
Koko
Notting Hill Arts Club
O2 Academy Brixton
Scala
Events
O2 Arena
Wembley
Jazz
Bull's Head, Barnes
The Jazz Café
Opera, Ballet and Concerts
Sadler's Wells Theatre
Wilton's Music Hall
Sport
All England Lawn Tennis Club, Wimbledon
Kia Oval
Lord's Cricket Ground
Wembley

EAT 140

British and Modern
The Glasshouse
European
Ottolenghi
Providores & Tapa Room
Gastropubs/Bars
The Gun

Shopping

Whether you're looking for the best local products, a department store or a quirky boutique, you'll find them all in London. In this section shops are listed alphabetically.

Introduction	**120**
Directory	**122**
Shopping A–Z	**123**

Introduction

If England really is a nation of shopkeepers, then London is the head office. You can find almost anything if you are determined enough. London has long been the world's marketplace and you'll find saris and spices as easily as rare reggae records, depending on the district—it really pays to explore beyond the West End. For shoppers, the choice ranges from vibrant street markets to legendary department stores and from offbeat boutiques to smart galleries of paintings and antiques.

Contemporary and Traditional

It is the range that excites visitors, whether in cutting-edge contemporary, classics or antiques. London has outrageous fashion, bolstered by the annual crop of imaginative art-, fashion- and design-school graduates. By contrast, long-established shopping streets, such as Oxford Street and Kensington High Street, offer mass-market goods, while markets such as Camden Lock and Portobello Road are eclectic, ethnic and inexpensive.

Buying a London Memory

London's souvenirs range from tatty to tasteful. Ever since the Swinging Sixties, anything with a

BEST OF BRITISH

Take home some British souvenirs with a difference. You can buy beautifully crafted umbrellas and walking sticks from James Smith & Sons (✉ 53 New Oxford Street, WC1). For a good British cheese buy a Stilton, all ready and packed, from Paxton & Whitfield (✉ 93 Jermyn Street, SW1). If you want to try some British recipes go to Books for Cooks (✉ 4 Blenheim Crescent, W11) for a large selection of cookbooks. Tea addicts should head to The Tea House (✉ 15A Neal Street, WC2) for a choice of blends and some stylish teapots. For bespoke stationery and leather goods, Smythson (✉ 40 New Bond Street, W1) is the epitome of elegance.

Clockwise from top: The elegant arcades of Leadenhall Market; handmade shoes for sale in St. James's; one of the antiques shops in Camden Passage; the central well

Union Jack flag on it has sold well. For high quality, go to the museum shops. Gifts at the shop in Buckingham Palace Mews include the Queen Victoria range of china, a mini-crown for a charm bracelet or a guardsman mug. The Victoria and Albert Museum, British Museum and National Gallery also stock quality items inspired by their diverse collections—budget permitting, you can do a full-scale family gift shop at any of these. Tate Modern has fine handcrafted jewelry, while the Museum of London is particularly good for souvenirs and books about London. At the National Portrait Gallery, you will find books on historical figures and British history, as well as a good supply of postcards and posters.

The Ultimate British Buy

Go to St. James's or Knightsbridge to purchase traditional British-made goods such as tweed jackets, handmade shoes or delicate fragrances, elegant china, floral printed fabrics and cashmere sweaters. Visit Burlington Arcade (▷ panel below) for its specialist upscale shops in a historic setting. Burberry and Aquascutum are synonymous with raincoats. Harrods has been trading for some 150 years; Selfridges was the country's first department store; and Liberty fabrics are still exotic and luxurious. The January and July sales are major events on any serious shopper's calendar.

SHOP THE SHOP

Charles Dickens would recognize many London shops. Burlington Arcade, off Piccadilly, is an 18th-century covered shopping mall, with a liveried beadle to maintain decorum. Many shops display the royal insignia, showing that they supply members of the Royal Household with everything from brushes to jewels (www.royalwarrant.org). For instance, John Lobb (✉ 88 Jermyn Street, SW1) custom-makes shoes and boots for the royal family—and for you, at a price.

in Liberty; Lobb on St. James's Street, selling exclusive made-to-measure shoes; Fortnum & Mason in Piccadilly, renowned for its luxury foods and top-notch wines

Directory

Fleet Street to the Tower

Street Markets
Leadenhall Market
Petticoat Lane
Spitalfields Market

Covent Garden to Regent's Park

Art and Antiques
Grays Antiques Market
Books
Stanfords
Department Stores
Liberty
Selfridges
Fashion
Beauty Box
Brora
Browns
Burberry
Food and Drink
Rococo
Villandry
Health and Beauty
Neal's Yard Remedies
Homeware
Aram Designs Ltd
Designers Guild
Heal's
Thomas Goode Ltd
Toys
Benjamin Pollock's Toyshop
Hamleys

Westminster and St. James's

Art and Antiques
Agnews
Books
Hatchards
Department Stores
Fortnum & Mason
Fashion
Turnbull & Asser

Around Hyde Park

Department Stores
Harrods
Harvey Nichols
Peter Jones
Fashion
Jimmy Choo
Lulu Guinness

Farther Afield

Books
Books for Cooks
Fashion
Start London
Homeware
Contemporary Applied Arts
Shopping Centers
Westfield London
Street Markets
Bermondsey Antiques Market
Camden Markets

AGNEWS

www.agnewsgallery.com

This internationally renowned art gallery, in business since 1817, specializes in European Old Masters and British art from the 17th to the 20th centuries.

H6 6 St James's Place, SW1 020 7491 9219 Mon–Fri 9.30–5.30 Green Park

ARAM DESIGNS LTD

www.aram.co.uk

Aram's international modern designs are displayed on five floors. Stock includes furniture, lighting and glass.

K4 110 Drury Lane, WC2 020 7557 7557 Mon–Sat 10–6 (Thu til 7pm) Covent Garden

BENJAMIN POLLOCK'S TOYSHOP

www.pollocks-coventgarden.co.uk

Selling traditional toy theaters and collectible toys for adults and children, this toy shop is delightfully different.

K5 44 The Market, WC2 020 7234 0805 Mon–Wed 10.30–6, Thu–Sat 10.30–6.30, Sun 11–6 Covent Garden

BERMONDSEY ANTIQUES MARKET

Rise before dawn on a Friday and join the bargain-hunters. The market is best for small items.

R8 Bermondsey Square, SE1 020 7240 7405 Fri 6am–2pm London Bridge

PRIVATE GALLERIES

An indispensable tool to help you find out more about commercial art galleries in London is the excellent monthly *Galleries* magazine (www.galleries.co.uk), which is available free from most galleries. With its maps and specialist subject index, information can be called up by area as well as subject.

BOOKS FOR COOKS

www.booksforcooks.com

Browse the amazing selection of books about cooking and cuisine. Then head to the café, where recipes are tested, for some refreshments. Cookery classes are held in the demonstration kitchen.

Off map 4 Blenheim Crescent, W11 020 7221 1992 Tue–Sat 10–6. Closed last 3 weeks in Aug and 10 days over Christmas and New Year Ladbroke Grove

BRORA

www.brora.co.uk

Choose from cashmere in an array of shades for men, women and children. It is expensive, but the quality is superb.

K5 42 The Market, WC2 020 7836 6921 Mon–Sat 10–7, Sun 11–5 Covent Garden

BROWNS

www.brownsfashion.com

This boutique has long led the fashion pack, offering chic designs at grown-up prices.

F4 23–27 South Molton Street, W1 020 7514 0016 Mon–Sat 10–6.30 (Thu til 7pm) Bond Street

BURBERRY BEAUTY BOX

http://uk.burberry.com

A new concept store for this iconic British brand, featuring make-up, fragrance and fashion in eye-catching displays and digital innovations.

K5 3a The Market Building, WC2 020 3618 3982 Mon–Sat 10–8, Sun 12–6 Covent Garden

BOOKSHOP CAFÉS

Bookshop cafés to seek out include the cake shop connected by a passage in the history section of London Review Bookshop (✉ 14 Bury Place, WC1 ☎ 020 7269 9030) and the café on the 5th floor of Foyles' flagship store (✉ 107 Charing Cross Road, WC2 ☎ 020 7440 3207). Waterstone's superstore on Piccadilly boasts 5th View, a cocktail bar and grill with rooftop views.

CAMDEN MARKETS

www.camdenlock.net

This is a string of popular markets, famous for alternative and vintage fashion, crafts and food.

✚ Off map ✉ Camden High Street to Chalk Farm Road, NW1 ⏲ Daily 9.30–6 with more stalls at weekends 🚇 Camden Town, Chalk Farm

CONTEMPORARY APPLIED ARTS

www.caa.org.uk

For quality contemporary crafts, head to CAA, which is dedicated to promoting British artists.

✚ N6 ✉ 89 Southwark Street, SE1 ☎ 020 7620 0086 ⏲ Mon–Sat 10–6, Sun 11–5 🚇 Southwark, Borough

DESIGNERS GUILD

www.designersguild.com

Tricia Guild's store is a wonderland of exquisite design, with a range of modern china, glass and fabrics.

✚ F3 ✉ 76 Marylebone High Street, W1 ☎ 020 3301 5826 ⏲ Mon–Sat 10–6 (Thu 7pm), Sun 11–5 🚇 Baker Street

FORTNUM & MASON

www.fortnumandmason.com

Before venturing into London's premier grocer's shop, do not miss the clock, which has Messrs. Fortnum and Mason edging forward each hour. The shop-brand Fortnum's goods make perfectly delicious presents.

✚ H6 ✉ 181 Piccadilly, W1 ☎ 020 7734 8040 ⏲ Mon–Sat 10–8, Sun 11.30–6 🚇 Piccadilly Circus, Green Park

GRAYS ANTIQUES MARKET

www.graysantiques.com

High-quality goods ranging from silver to vintage fashion are sold by over 200 dealers.

✚ F5 ✉ 1–7 Davies Mews and 58 Davies Street, W1 ☎ 020 7629 7034 ⏲ Mon–Fri 10–6, Sat 11–5 🚇 Bond Street

HAMLEYS

www.hamleys.com

In business for over 250 years and probably the world's most famous toy shop, Hamleys has five action-packed floors.

✚ H5 ✉ 188-196 Regent Street, W1 ☎ 0371 704 1977 ⏲ Mon–Wed 1–8, Thu–Fri 10–9, Sat 9.30–9, Sun 12–6 🚇 Oxford Circus

HARRODS

www.harrods.com

This vast emporium contains just about everything anyone could want. Don't miss the food halls.

✚ D8 ✉ 87–135 Brompton Road, SW1 ☎ 020 7730 1234 ⏲ Mon–Sat 10–8, Sun 11.30–6 🚇 Knightsbridge

HARVEY NICHOLS

www.harveynichols.com

Harvey Nichols bags the title of London's classiest clothes shop. It also has a chic, popular restaurant.

✚ E7 ✉ 109–125 Knightsbridge, SW1 ☎ 020 7235 5000 ⏲ Mon–Sat 10–8, Sun 11.30–6 🚇 Knightsbridge

HATCHARDS

www.hatchards.co.uk

Booksellers since 1797, the oldest bookshop in London and still in its original building, Hatchards' staff know how to make book-buying a rewarding experience.

H6 187 Piccadilly, W1 020 7439 9921 Mon–Sat 9.30–7, Sun 12–6 Piccadilly Circus, Green Park

HEAL'S

www.heals.co.uk

A front-runner of the 1920s Arts and Crafts movement, Heal's specializes in timeless, modern furniture and homewares.

J3 196 Tottenham Court Road, W1 020 7636 1666 Mon–Sat 10–7, Thu 10–8, Sun 12–6 Goodge Street

JIGSAW

www.jigsaw-online.com

Affordable design classics in the colours and fabrics of the moment, feature in this stylish British fashion chain's light, airy and elegant store.

E9 6 Duke of York's Square, SW3 020 7730 4404 Mon–Sat 10–7 (Wed 7.30pm), Sun 12–6 Sloane Square

JIMMY CHOO

www.jimmychoo.com

A fashionista heaven, Jimmy Choo in Knightsbridge is the place to buy the highest-heeled shoes in the latest styles in town.

E7 32 Sloane Street, SW3 020 7823 1051 Mon–Sat 10–6 (Wed 7pm), Sun 12–5 Knightsbridge

LEADENHALL MARKET

www.cityoflondon.gov.uk

This surprising City treat is housed under architect Horace Jones's elegant 19th-century arcades. Quality food shops, fashion boutiques, pubs and restaurants sit behind traditional shop fronts on cobbled streets under soaring glass roofs.

R4 Leadenhall, EC3 Mon–Fri 10–5 Bank, Monument

AUCTION HOUSES

A visit to one of London's auction houses, even just to view, is an experience. Try Bonham's (101 New Bond Street, W1 020 7447 7447, www.bonhams.com), Christie's (8 King Street, SW1 020 7839 9060, www.christies.com) or Sotheby's (34 New Bond Street, W1 020 7293 5000, www.sothebys.com).

Vibrant Camden Lock Market

MAKE A PICNIC

With so many parks and benches, London is a great place to picnic. The big stores have seductive food halls and stock wine; see Harrods, Selfridges and Fortnum & Mason. Old Compton Street is a food shopper's delight; see also Clarke's Bakery (✉ 122 Kensington Church Street, W8) and other cafés that sell pre-prepared food to take out.

LIBERTY

www.liberty.co.uk

With everything from sumptuous fabrics to china and glass, this shop is characterized by exoticism and cutting-edge fashion, with an Arts and Crafts heritage.

✚ G4 ✉ Regent Street, W1 ☎ 020 7734 1234 ⏲ Mon–Sat 10–8, Sun 12–6 🚇 Oxford Circus

LULU GUINNESS

www.luluguinness.com

Selling 1950s-style handbags, hats and shoes, this sleek, modern shop is popular with celebrities. Also found in Burlington Arcade and in the City's Royal Exchange.

✚ E9 ✉ 3 Ellis Street, SW1 ☎ 020 7823 4828 ⏲ Mon–Sat 10–6 🚇 Sloane Square

NEAL'S YARD REMEDIES

www.nealsyardremedies.com

Committed to using natural ingredients in its products, Neal's Yard health and beauty shop is a Covent Garden institution.

✚ K4 ✉ 15 Neal's Yard, WC2 ☎ 020 7379 7222 ⏲ Mon–Sat 10–7, Sun 11–6 🚇 Covent Garden

PETER JONES

www.johnlewis.com

This department store sells everything from designer labels to homewares, while there are great views from the café and cocktail bar.

✚ E9 ✉ Sloane Square, SW1 ☎ 020 7730 3434 ⏲ Mon–Sat 9.30–7 (Wed 8), Sun 12–6 🚇 Sloane Square

PETTICOAT LANE

This is the place for clothing at bargain prices. It is best on Sunday.

✚ S4 ✉ Middlesex and Wentworth streets, E1 ⏲ Mon–Fri 8–4, Sun 9–2 🚇 Liverpool Street, Aldgate

ROCOCO

www.rococochocolates.com

The chocolates at this upscale chocolatier offer a taste sensation that's packed with style.

✚ F3 ✉ 3 Moxon Street, W1 ☎ 020 7935 7780 ⏲ Tue–Sat 10–6.30, Sun–Mon 11–6 🚇 Baker Street, Regents Park

ROYAL EXCHANGE

www.theroyalexchange.co.uk

William Tite's City landmark is now a beautiful upscale shopping mall.

✚ Q4 ✉ Cornhill ⏲ Mon–Fri 10–6; restaurants and bars 8am–11pm 🚇 Bank

SELFRIDGES

www.selfridges.com

The main rival to Harvey Nichols (▷ 124) for daylong retail therapy. Don't miss the superb food hall.

✚ F4 ✉ 400 Oxford Street, W1 ☎ 0800 123 400 ⏲ Mon–Sat 9.30–9, Sun 11.30–6.15 🚇 Marble Arch, Bond Street

SPITALFIELDS MARKET

www.oldspitalfieldsmarket.com

Wander among the craft stalls and array of food outlets. The Saturday Style Market attracts designers.

✚ S3 ✉ Crispin Place, E1 ☎ 020 7375 2963 ⏲ Mon–Fri, Sat 11–5, Sun 10–5 🚇 Liverpool Street

START LONDON

www.start-london.com

Hot his-and-hers designer fashion across three smart stores in trendy Shoreditch.

Off map at R2 40, 42 and 59 Rivington Street, EC2 020 7729 3334 Daily High Street Kensington

STANFORDS

www.stanfords.co.uk

With London's largest selection of maps, plus travel books and a good little café, Stanfords is a must for all travel enthusiasts.

K5 12–14 Long Acre, WC2 020 7836 1321 Mon–Fri 10.30–6.30 (Thu 7), Sat 11–6, Sun 11–5 Old Street

THOMAS GOODE LTD

www.thomasgoode.com

Collectors of bone china, fine glassware and cutlery need look no further than this splendid showroom. Styles range from contemporary and classic to ultimate luxury.

F5 19 South Audley Street, W1 020 7499 2823 Mon–Sat 10–6 Green Park, Bond Street

TURNBULL & ASSER

www.turnbullandasser.co.uk

If you want classic British design, then the made-to-measure or off-the-peg shirts here are for you. Quality and service are superb.

H6 71–72 Jermyn Street, SW1 020 7808 3000 Mon–Fri 9–6, Sat 9.30–6 Green Park, Piccadilly Circus

VILLANDRY

www.villandry.com

This quality foodstore sells a superb range of French and English cheeses, great breads, olive oil, charcuterie and more.

G3 170 Great Portland Street, W1 020 7631 3131 Mon–Fri 7.30–10.30, Sat 8–10.30, Sun 9–6 Great Portland Street

SHOPPING SECRETS

For streets full of character, try Blenheim Crescent in Notting Hill, W11; Kensington Church Street, W8, renowned for its antiques shops and galleries, and Marylebone High Street, W1, which delights with food, fashion and Oxfam's flagship books and music shop. Secreted off Oxford Street, Gees Court and St. Christopher's Place are fashion favorites.

WESTFIELD LONDON

http://uk.westfield.com/london

With over 300 shops spanning designer and high-street labels, department stores and boutiques, Westfield provides all-day shopping. There are plenty of cafés and restaurants to sustain shoppers, too. The larger Westfield Stratford City is located by the Olympic site.

Off map Ariel Way, W12 020 3371 2300 Shepherd's Bush, Wood Lane

Liberty's mock-Tudor main entrance

GARRICK
ENCHANTING
EXQUISITE

Entertainment

Once you've done with sightseeing for the day, you'll find lots of other great things to do with your time in this chapter, even if all you want to do is relax with a drink. In this section establishments are listed alphabetically.

Introduction	**130**
Directory	**132**
Entertainment A–Z	**133**

Introduction

When darkness falls, London's pace doesn't let up, and there's a huge choice of lively nightclubs, bars and pubs where you can mingle with the locals.

Entertainment

London's Theatreland, with its lavish West End musicals and plays starring A-list actors, is famed worldwide, but there's a great deal happening in smaller venues all over town, including alternative theater, comedy and cabaret. Hundreds of concerts take place every week in a variety of buildings, but especially churches, where the quality of lunchtime and evening recitals is very high and admission is either nominal or free. London's newest cultural landmark is King's Place (tel 020 7520 1440, www.kingsplace.co.uk) in the revitalized area of King's Cross. There are opera, ballet and modern dance seasons in memorable locations, too, plus an array of fun festivals, especially during the summer months and the long public holiday weekends.

Film

As well as the big-screen cinemas in the West End showing the latest blockbuster movies, London has some very good venues screening art-house and indie films. The BFI Southbank

WALK THE WALK

The 2km-long (1 mile) stretch of riverside on the South Bank between Westminster Bridge and London Bridge bustles by night, as well as by day. The London Eye is magical after dusk. On the opposite bank, illuminated landmarks include the Houses of Parliament and Somerset House. At Oxo Tower Wharf, go to the top floor for a drink or a meal—there are few better views of London. Admire Tate Modern (open until 10pm Friday and Saturday) and the Globe. Rest your feet at a riverside pub and enjoy spectacular views.

Clockwise from top: The Garrick Theatre in the West End; the Theatre Royal on Haymarket; the BFI IMAX on the South Bank; Shakespeare's Globe, a re-creation of

(▷ 133), which hosts the annual London Film Festival in October, Ciné Lumière (▷ 134), the Electric Cinema in Notting Hill (www.electriccinema.co.uk), the Curzon Mayfair and Renoir in the Brunswick Centre (both www.curzoncinemas.com) are all well worth visiting.

Summer Living

In the summer, London's outdoors comes into its own. Londoners enjoy concerts in beautiful settings such as Hampton Court Palace, Kenwood House, Hyde Park and Kew Gardens, often bringing picnics with them. The music ranges from classical and opera to jazz and rock. Bars, pubs and cafés spill onto the city's streets, and many serve good food.

Clubs, Pubs and Bars

Year-round, the diversity of the club scene is legendary and, with many changing themes, check before you go. There are tried-and-tested venues and a host of pulsing new wave options. London's extensive bar scene ranges from cocktails at the elegant Savoy (▷ 159) or the see-and-be-seen Blue Bar at The Berkeley (▷ 156) to Irish bars, sports bars and traditional street-corner pubs. You'll find some are in warrens of Tudor rooms; others take pride in their Victorian and Edwardian decorations.

LANDMARK CLUBBING

A mix of global names, trailblazing bands and DJs make Xoyo (✉ 32–37 Cowper Street, EC2 ☎ 020 7354 9993, www.xoyo.co.uk) a popular Shoreditch venue. The Nest (✉ 36–44 Stoke Newington Road, N16, www.ilovethenest.com) promises a soundtrack that covers everything from house and garage to disco, techno and trap from cutting-edge new talent. Under Blackfriars Bridge, Pulse (✉ Invicta Plaza, SE1 ☎ 020 7261 0981, www.pulseclub.co.uk) is London's largest state-of-the-art club space, with hi-tech sound and video mapping.

an Elizabethan playhouse; Young Dancer, *a bronze by Enzo Plazzotta outside the Royal Opera House in Covent Garden*

South Bank

Clubs
Ministry of Sound
Film
BFI IMAX
BFI Southbank
Opera, Ballet and Concerts
Purcell Room
Queen Elizabeth Hall
Royal Festival Hall
Theaters
National Theatre
Old Vic
Shakespeare's Globe
Young Vic

Fleet Street to the Tower

Clubs
Fabric
Events
Broadgate Centre
Opera, Ballet and Concerts
Barbican Concert Hall
Theaters
Barbican Centre Theatre

Covent Garden to Regent's Park

Clubs
The Borderline
Guanabara
Salsa!
Jazz
Jazz After Dark
Pizza Express Jazz Club Soho
Opera, Ballet and Concerts
London Coliseum
Royal Opera House
Wigmore Hall
Theaters
Donmar Warehouse
Theatre Royal, Drury Lane

Westminster to St. James's

Comedy
The Comedy Store
Dancing
The Ritz
Film
Institute of Contemporary Arts (ICA)
Opera, Ballet and Concerts
St. James's, Piccadilly
St. Martin-in-the-Fields

Around Hyde Park

Film
Ciné Lumière
Opera, Ballet and Concerts
Cadogan Hall
Holland Park Theatre
Royal Albert Hall
Theaters
Royal Court/Jerwood Theatre Upstairs

Farther Afield

Clubs
606 Club
Barfly
Bush Hall
Forum
Koko
Notting Hill Arts Club
O2 Academy Brixton
Scala
Events
O2 Arena
Jazz
Bull's Head, Barnes
The Jazz Café
Opera, Ballet and Concerts
Sadler's Wells Theatre
Wilton's Music Hall
Sport
All England Lawn Tennis Club, Wimbledon
Kia Oval
Lord's Cricket Ground
Wembley

Entertainment A-Z

606 CLUB

www.606club.co.uk

West London's best small jazz club books musicians with impeccable credentials. Alcohol is served only with food and the music cover charge is added to the cost of the meal.

Off map 90 Lots Road, SW10 020 7352 5953 Mon–Thu 7pm–1am, Fri–Sat 8pm–2am, Sun 7–11pm Earl's Court then bus C3, Fulham Broadway

ALL ENGLAND LAWN TENNIS CLUB, WIMBLEDON

www.wimbledon.com

In late June, line up for tickets to tennis's top tournament (advance tickets only for the last four days). Tours and museum entrance are available all year.

Off map Church Road, SW19 Tours: 020 8946 6131 Southfields

BARBICAN CENTRE THEATRE

www.barbican.org.uk

Currently an exciting mix of domestic and international companies play seasons here.

P3 Barbican Centre, Silk Street, EC2 020 7638 8891 Barbican

BARBICAN CONCERT HALL

www.barbican.org.uk.

Home to the London Symphony Orchestra and the BBC Symphony Orchestra, the Barbican also welcomes visiting orchestras, singers and soloists.

R3 Barbican Centre, Silk Street, EC2 020 7638 8891; range of good ticket deals Barbican

BARFLY

http://thebarflylondon.com

A Camden club that hosts more than 20 indie groups a week—some bad, some OK and some destined for stardom.

Off map 49 Chalk Farm Road, NW1 020 7424 0800 Mon, Thu 3pm–2am, Tue–Wed 3pm–1am, Fri–Sat 3pm–3am, Sun 3pm–midnight Chalk Farm

BFI IMAX

www.bfi.org.uk/bfi-imax

Watch exhilarating 2-D and 3-D movies in this 500-seat cinema in a space-age setting.

L6 1 Charlie Chaplin Walk, South Bank, SE1 0330 333 7878 Embankment, Waterloo

BFI SOUTHBANK

www.bfi.org.uk

BFI Southbank screens a diverse range of films and is the focus of the annual London Film Festival.

L6 South Bank, SE1 020 7928 3232 Embankment, Waterloo

THE BORDERLINE

http://theborderlinelondon.com

The hottest indie and rock bands strut their stuff at the venerable Borderline club in the West End.

J4 Orange Yard, off Manette Street, W1 020 7734 5547 Concerts: 7–11pm; Clubs and special events 11pm–3 or 4am Tottenham Court Road

THEATER TIPS

If you care about where you sit, you can usually find a seating plan online. For an evening "sold out" performance, it is worth waiting in line for returns; otherwise, try for a matinée. The cheapest seats may be far from the stage or uncomfortable, so take binoculars and a cushion. Londoners rarely dress up for the theater but they do order their intermission drinks before the play starts, and usually remain seated while they applaud.

MUSIC EVERYWHERE!

London is full of music. At lunchtime, the best places are churches, where concerts are usually free. Try St. Anne and St. Agnes, and St. Olave's in the City; St. James's, Piccadilly; and St. Martin-in-the-Fields in Trafalgar Square. St. Paul's Cathedral has choral evensong at 5pm Monday to Saturday, 3.15 on Sunday. Look for concerts in historic houses, museums and galleries, especially during the City of London Festival (July). On summer evenings music is played outside in the Embankment Gardens or at Kenwood House (▷ 77).

The famed Comedy Store

BROADGATE CENTRE

www.broadgate.co.uk

This amphitheater, surrounded by bars, restaurants and shops, provides a schedule of summer entertainment and a winter ice rink.

R3 Broadgate Circus, Eldon Street, EC2 020 7505 5310 Liverpool Street

BULL'S HEAD, BARNES

www.thebullshead.com

Enjoy good jazz in the friendly atmosphere of a riverside pub.

Off map 373 Lonsdale Road, SW13 020 8876 5241 Mon–Fri 11am–11pm, Sat 12–11, Sun 12–10; jazz nightly from 8 Barnes Bridge

BUSH HALL

www.bushhallmusic.co.uk

Listen to jazz, rock, folk or classics performed by famous names and upcoming artists at this ornate Edwardian dance hall.

Off map 310 Uxbridge Road, Shepherd's Bush, W12 020 8222 6955 Shows: 7.30pm, see website for listings Shepherd's Bush Market

CADOGAN HALL

www.cadoganhall.com

This concert hall off Sloane Square is home to the Royal Philharmonic Orchestra. It also welcomes visiting musicians and vocalists.

E9 5 Sloane Terrace, SW1 020 7730 4500 Sloane Square

CINÉ LUMIÈRE

www.institut-francais.org.uk/cine-lumiere/

Part of the French government's hub of language and culture, Ciné Lumière shows French films and other European and world cinema.

B9 Institut Français, 17 Queensberry Place, SW7 020 7871 3535 Closed Aug South Kensington

THE COMEDY STORE

www.thecomedystore.co.uk

The best in stand-up comedy features improvised sketches from the Comedy Store Players. Many big names in British TV and radio have cut their teeth here.

J5 1a Oxendon Street, SW1 Doors open Mon–Thu at 6.30pm, Fri–Sun 6pm. Show times vary, check website for details Piccadilly Circus, Leicester Square

DONMAR WAREHOUSE

www.donmarwarehouse.com

The Donmar Warehouse attracts adventurous theatergoers to its avant-garde productions.

J4 41 Earlham Street, WC2 Covent Garden

FABRIC

www.fabriclondon.com

This fabulously cool superclub is known for its music blasted out in three rooms and is hugely popular.

N3 77a Charterhouse Street, EC1 020 7336 8898 Fri–Sun from 11pm Farringdon

THE FORUM

http://theforumlondon.com

Live music in a thirties' art deco theatre featuring indie bands, hip hop and metal.

Off map 9–17 Highgate Road, NW5 020 7428 4080 See website for listings and times Kentish Town

GUANABARA

www.guanabara.co.uk

Grab a caipirinha and salsa onto the dance floor at this Brazilian-themed venue. Tables must be booked in advance.

K4 Parker Street, WC2 020 7242 8600 Tue 5pm–1am, Wed–Sat 5pm–2.30am, Sun 6pm–midnight Covent Garden, Holborn

HOLLAND PARK THEATRE

www.operahollandpark.com

Confusingly, this is highly acclaimed opera, not theater, staged in summer (June to August) beneath a canopy in one of London's most romantic parks.

Off map Holland Park, W8 0300 999 1000 Holland Park, High Street Kensington

INSTITUTE OF CONTEMPORARY ARTS (ICA)

www.ica.org.uk

Founded by a collective of artists, poets and writers, the Institute of Contemporary Arts hosts cutting-edge art, screens seriously arty films and plays host to performance artists charting new territory in all media.

J6 The Mall, SW1 020 7930 3647 Tue–Sun 11–11; exhibitions 11–6, Thu 11–9 (see website for listings) Piccadilly Circus, Charing Cross

JAZZ AFTER DARK

www.jazzafterdark.co.uk

Jazz and blues attract a keen young crowd. The cocktails are good and the food simple. By day it's an art gallery.

J4 9 Greek Street, W1 020 7734 0545 Tue–Thu 5pm–2am (live music from 9pm), Fri–Sat 5pm–3am (live music from 10.30pm) Tottenham Court Road

THE JAZZ CAFÉ

http://thejazzcafelondon.com

Buzzing nightly with the widest range of jazz, soul, R&B and funk, this has been a popular spot since it opened in the 1980s.

Off map 5 Parkway, NW1 020 7734 0545 Mon–Sun 7pm–2am Camden Town

ALL THAT JAZZ

London has a great concentration of world-class jazz musicians, both home-grown and foreign, traditional and contemporary. Evening and late-night gigs cover rock, roots, rhythm and blues and more, many in pubs. For a list of venues, check *Time Out*. Also, to get the latest information on jazz visit www.jazznights.co.uk.

KIA OVAL

www.kiaoval.com

The Oval is where Surrey County Cricket Club play home games. It is also a venue for test cricket and Sunday league games. You can also take a tour of the ground.

Off map Surrey County Cricket Club, Kennington, SE11 Oval

KOKO

www.koko.uk.com

Since 1890, this Camden Town venue has been through many incarnations. Today, go for hip-hop, trance, pop, rock and partying under the gigantic mirror ball.

Off map 1a Camden High Street, NW1 020 7388 3222 Sun–Thu 7pm–11.30pm, Fri 7pm–9.30pm. Club NME: Fri 9.30pm–4am, Sat 9pm–4am Mornington Crescent, Camden Town

LONDON COLISEUM

www.eno.org

The London Coliseum is home to the English National Opera (ENO), which is known for its exciting and innovative productions.

J5 St. Martin's Lane, WC2 020 7845 9300 Leicester Square, Charing Cross

TICKET TIPS

Use the TKTS half-price ticket booth (in Leicester Square). Preview tickets and matinée tickets have reduced prices. Many theater box offices sell cheaper tickets from 10am on the day of performance. Go with friends and make a party booking at a reduced rate. Ask the National Theatre, Royal Court and other theaters about special discounts on particular performances; and keep student and senior citizen cards ready. Remember, the show is the same wherever you sit!

LORD'S CRICKET GROUND

www.lords.org

Lords is the home of the MCC (Marylebone Cricket Club) and is where Middlesex play home games. The ground hosts test cricket, major finals and Sunday league games.

Off map St. John's Wood Road, NW8 020 7616 8500 St. John's Wood

MINISTRY OF SOUND

www.ministryofsound.com

This legendary club is housed in a prison-like building and stars world-class DJs.

N8 103 Gaunt Street, SE1 020 7740 8600 Fri 10.30pm–6am, Sat 11pm–7am (last entry 2 hours before closing) Elephant and Castle

NATIONAL THEATRE

www.nationaltheatre.org.uk

The home of the National Theatre company has three performance spaces: the Olivier, Lyttelton and Dorfman. All stage several productions in repertory.

L6 South Bank, SE1 020 7452 3000 Information, tickets and tours Embankment, Waterloo Waterloo

NOTTING HILL ARTS CLUB

www.nottinghillartsclub.com

Diversity and originality results from artists and DJs meeting here and swapping ideas.

Off map 21 Notting Hill Gate, W11 020 7460 4459 Times vary, check website for details Notting Hill Gate

O2 ACADEMY BRIXTON

www.o2academybrixton.co.uk

South London's favorite live music venue attracts big-name bands. It has an art deco interior and room for nearly 5,000 on the

BACKSTAGE TOURS

The Royal Opera House, Covent Garden (www.roh.org.uk) has 90-minute backstage tours and a 45-minute Velvet, Gilt and Glamour tour. Front-of-house tours of the Royal Albert Hall (www.royalalberthall.com) last an hour and the guides have some great stories. The National Theatre tours are always highly praised (www.nationaltheatre.org.uk), and actors reveal history at the Theatre Royal, Drury Lane (www.theatreroyaldrurylane.com). The Globe, the London Palladium and London Coliseum also offers tours.

huge sloping dance floor. All the big rock bands have played and recorded here.
Off map 211 Stockwell Road, SW9 020 7771 3000 Times vary, check website for details Brixton, Stockwell

O2 ARENA

www.theo2.co.uk
A music and sports venue in the former Millennium Dome, the O2 Arena has a capacity of 20,000.
Off map Peninsula Square, SE10 020 8463 2000 North Greenwich

OLD VIC

www.oldvictheatre.com
This sumptuous theater stages critically acclaimed productions.
M7 The Cut, Waterloo Road, SE1 Waterloo, Southwark

PIZZA EXPRESS JAZZ CLUB SOHO

www.pizzaexpresslive.com
Savor quality pizzas and great jazz in this friendly Soho cellar (booking is essential).
J4 10 Dean Street, W1 Tottenham Court Road

PURCELL ROOM

www.southbankcentre.co.uk
Listen to chamber music, singers, musicians, poets and more in this intimate space.
L6 South Bank, SE1 Embankment, Waterloo

QUEEN ELIZABETH HALL

www.southbankcentre.co.uk
Come here for small orchestras, choirs, small-scale opera, piano recitals and dance.
L6 South Bank, SE1 Embankment, Waterloo

THE RITZ

www.theritzlondon.com
To enter a bygone world, dress up for dinner and a dance on a Friday or Saturday at London's most opulent dining room (booking essential). For a more modest experience, go for afternoon tea in the Palm Court or the Rivoli Bar.
G6 150 Piccadilly, W1 020 7493 8181 Green Park

ROYAL ALBERT HALL

www.royalalberthall.com
Sporting events fill the 6,000-seat hall as well as concerts, opera and the annual Henry Wood Promenade Concerts, which runs from mid-July to mid-September, offering nightly concerts and cheap "proms" tickets for audiences to stand on the floor of the pit.
B7 Kensington Gore, SW7 South Kensington

ROYAL COURT/JERWOOD THEATRE UPSTAIRS

www.royalcourttheatre.com
The Royal Court has a lofty artistic reputation and presents only new

work by leading or emerging playwrights. In the 1950s, John Osbourne's *Look Back In Anger* shook up London theater forever, and today's productions follow in its wake. The main theater seats 370, the studio 85.
E9 Sloane Square, SW1 020 7565 5000 Sloane Square

ROYAL FESTIVAL HALL
www.southbankcentre.co.uk
The Royal Festival Hall, at the heart of the South Bank Centre arts complex, stages world-class performances, with large-scale orchestral concerts, plus jazz and ballet.
L6 South Bank, SE1
Embankment, Waterloo

ROYAL OPERA HOUSE
www.roh.org.uk
The opulent Royal Opera House in Covent Garden is home to the Royal Ballet and is an evocative setting for grand opera.
K5 Bow Street, Covent Garden, WC2
020 7304 4000 Covent Garden

SADLER'S WELLS THEATRE
www.sadlerswells.com
Sadler's Wells is one of the most electrifying dance theaters in Europe, with an exciting array of international and British companies presenting innovative dance of all genres with exciting choreography and performances.
M1 Rosebery Avenue, EC1
Angel

ST. JAMES'S, PICCADILLY
www.sjp.org.uk
This mid-17th-century church by Sir Christopher Wren's makes a sumptuous setting for lunchtime and evening choral and orchestral concerts, plus star lecturers.
H6 197 Piccadilly, W1 020 7734 4511 Piccadilly Circus

ST. MARTIN-IN-THE-FIELDS
www.stmartin-in-the-fields.org
Baroque music is the focus of the free lunchtime concerts (Monday, Tuesday and Friday) and candlelit evening concerts (Thursday to Saturday). There are also jazz nights in the crypt, where there's a café/restaurant.
K5 Trafalgar Square, WC2 020 7766 1100 Charing Cross

SALSA!
www.bar-salsa.com
Come here for a salsa class held in the bar, then dance the night away or enjoy great Latin American food.
J5 96 Charing Cross Road, WC2
020 7379 3277 Sun–Thu 5pm–2am, Fri–Sat 5pm–3am Tottenham Court Road, Leicester Square

SCALA
www.scala-london.co.uk
This King's Cross superclub is spread over four main floors, with

PUB MUSIC

This can be one of the least expensive and most enjoyable evenings out in London, and worth the trip to an offbeat location. For the price of a pint of beer (usually a huge choice) you can settle down to enjoy the ambience and listen to some of the best alternative music available in town—from folk, jazz and blues to rhythm and blues, soul and much more. Audiences tend to be friendly, loyal to their venue and happy to talk music.

a viewing gallery. Music is provided by DJs and live bands.
Off map 282 Pentonville Road, N1 020 7833 2022 Live music nights: 7.30pm–11pm. Club nights: 9pm–3am King's Cross

SHAKESPEARE'S GLOBE
www.shakespearesglobe.com
The performance season at this reconstruction of an open-air Elizabethan playhouse runs May to September; take a coat and rainhat to watch works by Shakespeare and his contemporaries. Tours operate year-round (▷ 48).
P6 21 New Globe Walk, SE1 020 7401 9919 London Bridge, Mansion House, Blackfriars, Southwark

THEATRE ROYAL, DRURY LANE
www.theatreroyaldrurylane.com
The theater, built in 1812, stages mostly musicals. It is believed to be haunted—the Man in Grey is said to walk around the Upper Circle.
K5 Catherine Street, WC2 Covent Garden

WEMBLEY
www.wembleystadium.com
www.livenation.co.uk/wembley
The state-of-the art football stadium, where the English national team plays home games, also hosts big-name pop and rock concerts.
Off map Stadium Way, Wembley, Middlesex 0800 169 2007 Wembley Park Wembley Stadium

WIGMORE HALL
www.wigmore-hall.org.uk
The hall was built in 1901 as a recital hall for Bechstein Pianos, so it has perfect acoustics. It is one of London's most beautiful settings for recitals and chamber music, especially for Sunday concerts.
F4 36 Wigmore Street, W1 020 7935 2141 Bond Street

A production at Shakespeare's Globe

WILTON'S MUSIC HALL
http://wiltons.org.uk
The world's oldest surviving Grand Music Hall may be hard to find (a door in the wall of a pedestrian alley), but it's worth it. An atmospheric arts and heritage venue that, like the East End around it, is experiencing revival after hard times, its innovative and diverse offering includes classical music, cabaret, opera, dance and magic.
Off map at S5 1 Grace's Alley (off Ensign Street), E1 020 3468 5670 Check website for listings Aldgate East, Tower Hill

YOUNG VIC
www.youngvic.org
Young directors stage innovative productions of classic and new plays and musicals here.
M7 The Cut, SE1 020 7922 2922 Waterloo, Southwark

Eat

There are places to eat across the city to suit all tastes and budgets. In this section establishments are listed alphabetically.

Introduction	**142**
Directory	**143**
Eating A–Z	**144**

Introduction

With more than 50 restaurants awarded one or more Michelin stars, the capital's reputation for fine dining continues to grow. Chefs have high profiles and London creates its own culinary trends. Using the finest-quality ingredients, modern British cuisine values simplicity and flavor, innovation and elegant presentation.

Cafés, Brasseries and Pubs

Multicultural London offers exciting restaurants serving a wide variety of different cuisines, ranging from European and cutting-edge contemporary to Indian, Asian and Middle Eastern. Tapas and sushi bars are popular and you don't have to look far to find a good spicy curry or fragrant Thai treat. No longer just an excuse to rest your feet, museum and art gallery cafés are as much of a destination as their exhibitions and, with their all-day menus, convivial brasseries have a relaxed Continental air. Gastropubs combine a fine setting with quality drinks and food.

Fast Food and Restaurant Chains

Try the Gourmet Burger Kitchen, Yo!Sushi, Wagamama, All-Bar-One and Masala Zone. Zizzi and Pizza Express are good pizza chains.

Afternoon Tea

A great British institution, afternoon tea is still available in hotels and tearooms from about 2 or 3pm. It always includes a pot of tea and something to eat, which can vary from dainty sandwiches and cakes to scones with clotted cream and jam.

DRESS CODE

In the past the British loved to dress for dinner, but these days only the most formal restaurants demand a jacket and tie. Customers should dress appropriately, however, to eat in upscale restaurants.

Top to bottom: The Palm Court at the Ritz; summertime alfresco dining in the capital; focaccia for sale at Borough Market; artisan breads, Borough Market

Directory

South Bank

British and Modern
Oxo Tower Bar, Brasserie & Restaurant
European
Baltic
Gastropubs/Bars
The Anchor
Anchor & Hope
Lighter Bites
Tate Modern Café

Fleet Street to the Tower

Asian
Banh Mi Bay
British and Modern
The Café Below
Medcalf
Restaurant at St. Paul's
St. John
European
Bevis Marks Restaurant
Club Gascon
Famous Chefs
Fifteen
Gastropubs/Bars
The Peasant

Covent Garden to Regent's Park

Asian
Benares
Chaopraya Eat-Thai
Masala Zone
Rasa W1
Brasseries/Brunch
Christopher's
Joe Allen
British and Modern
Rules
European
Gaby's Deli
Hibiscus
Icebar London
Villandry
Wild Honey
Famous Chefs
The Square
Tom's Kitchen
Gastropubs/Bars
The Dog and Duck
Lowlander Grand Café
International
Ceviche
Lighter Bites
Paul
Vegetarian
Food for Thought
Wild Food Café

Westminster and St. James's

Asian
Tamarind
British and Modern
Portrait Restaurant
The Wolseley
Famous Chefs
Le Gavroche
Greenhouse
International
Gaucho
Lighter Bites
Inn the Park

Around Hyde Park

Asian
Amaya
Royal China
British and Modern
Babylon
Bibendum
Maggie Jones's
Famous Chefs
Maze
Lighter Bites
The Orangery

Farther Afield

British and Modern
The Glasshouse
European
Ottolenghi
La Poule au Pot
Providores & Tapa Room
Gastropubs/Bars
The Gun

PRICES

Prices are approximate, based on a 3-course meal for one person.

£££	over £60
££	£30–£60
£	under £30

AMAYA ££–£££

www.amaya.biz

Enjoy sophisticated Indian grills and curries in a modern, vibrant and upscale setting complete with a theatrical show kitchen.

E8 Halkin Arcade, Motcomb Street, SW1 020 7823 1166 Mon–Sat 12.30–2.15, 6.30–11.30, Sun 12.45–2.45, 6.30–10.30 Knightsbridge

THE ANCHOR £

This historic pub with its black beams, a maze of tiny rooms and pleasant garden terrace enjoys excellent river views. Food is traditional British, with fish and chips and Sunday roasts.

P6 Bankside, 34 Park Street, SE1

RIVERSIDE EATING

London is exploiting the potential of its riverside views. As well as traditional pubs such as The Anchor (▷ above) many new restaurants are opening along the South Bank. The most spectacular views are from the Oxo Tower Restaurant (▷ 149) and Tate Modern's rooftop restaurant at Bankside (▷ 151). There are lower but impressive views from the collection of eateries that line the Thames in the Southbank Centre (▷ 83). The Pilgrim Fathers' ship moored on the site of the Mayflower, London's oldest Thameside pub (117 Rotherhithe Street, SE16). Go for history, tradition and river views.

020 7407 1577 Restaurant: Mon–Sat 12–10, Sun 12–9 London Bridge

ANCHOR & HOPE ££

A quality gastropub serving good British food. There are no reservations (except for Sunday lunch) so arrive early or be prepared for a wait in the bar.

M7 36 The Cut, SE1 020 7928 9898 Tue–Sat 11–11, Mon 5–11, Sun 12.30–3.15 Southwark, Waterloo

BABYLON ££–£££

www.roofgardens.virgin.com

Take a seat in the rooftop gardens, complete with oak trees, flamingos and expansive views over London, for elegant modern British cuisine. Being there is a great experience.

Off map The Roof Garden, 99 Kensington High Street, W8 020 7368 3993 Mon–Sat 12–2.30, 7–10.30, Sun 12–4 High Street Kensington

BANH MI BAY £

Bright and light Vietnamese diner in a country-kitchen style that's popular with local workers at lunchtime (it does take-outs, too). The authentic dishes are delicious and good value.

L3 4–6 Theobalds Road, Holborn, WC1 020 7404 4016 Mon–Fri 11–4, 5.30–9.45, Sat 12–9.45 Chancery Lane

BALTIC £

www.balticrestaurant.co.uk

Head to the bar for some serious cocktails, then on to the dramatic contemporary restaurant for modern Polish and Eastern European food and jazz every Sunday 7pm.

N6 74 Blackfriars Road, SE1 020 7928 1111 Restaurant: Mon–Sat 5.30–11.15, Tue–Sat lunch 12–3, Sun 12–4.30, 5.30–10.30. Bar: 12–12 Southwark

AMERICAN EXPERIENCE

America's fast food arrived long before its quality cuisine and restaurant style became established. Better burger bars include The Ultimate Burger and Gourmet Burger Kitchen chains. Upscale options include Joe Allen (▷ 148), Christopher's (▷ below) and PJ's (✉ 52 Fulham Road, SW3 ☎ 020 7581 0025). Other good-value places to hang out are The Big Easy (✉ 332–4 King's Road, SW3 ☎ 020 7352 4071), Bodeans (✉ 10 Poland Street, W1 ☎ 020 7287 7575), The Hard Rock Café (✉ 150 Old Park Lane, W1 ☎ 020 7514 1700) and Automat (✉ 33 Dover Street, W1 ☎ 020 7499 3033).

BENARES £££

www.benaresrestaurant.com

Atul Kochhar serves subtly spiced and stylish Indian dishes in his Michelin-starred Mayfair restaurant. The menu is seasonally inspired, with innovative vegetarian options.

✚ G5 ✉ 12a Berkeley Square House, Berkeley Square, W1 ☎ 020 7629 8886 ⏲ Mon–Sat 12–2.30, 5.30–11 🚇 Green Park

BEVIS MARKS RESTAURANT ££

www.bevismarkstherestaurant.com

You'll find elegant dining at this highly rated kosher restaurant, with Israeli, and other, wines on offer.

✚ R4 ✉ 3 Middlesex Street, E1 ☎ 020 7427 5474 ⏲ Mon–Fri 12–3, Mon–Thu 5.30–10.30 🚇 Aldgate

BIBENDUM ££–£££

www.bibendum.co.uk

In a landmark building with art-nouveau elegance and charm, enjoy classic French food with British flair in the restaurant or go for relaxed luxury in the Oyster Bar.

✚ D9 ✉ 81 Fulham Road, SW3 ☎ 020 7581 5817 ⏲ Mon–Fri 12–2.30, 7–11, Sat–Sun 12.30–3, 7–10.30 (Sat 11); Oyster Bar daily 12–11 (Sun 10.30) 🚇 South Kensington

THE CAFÉ BELOW £

www.cafebelow.co.uk

In the medieval crypt of a Wren church with walls dating back to before 1066, you'll find fresh seasonal ingredients on British-, French- and Mediterranean-influenced menus.

✚ P4 ✉ St. Mary-le-Bow, Cheapside, EC2 ☎ 020 7329 0789 ⏲ Mon–Tue 7.30am–2.30pm, Wed–Fri 7.30am–9pm 🚇 Bank, St. Paul's, Mansion House

CEVICHE £–££

www.cevicheuk.com

Peruvian food is the big new taste sensation and Ceviche is the hot London source of this tasty and healthy cuisine.

✚ J4 ✉ 17 Frith Street, W1 ☎ 020 7292 2040 ⏲ Mon–Sat 12–11.30, Sun 12–10.15 🚇 Tottenham Court Road, Leicester Square, Piccadilly Circus

CHAOPRAYA EAT-THAI ££

www.eatthai.net

Enjoy classic Thai dishes at this quiet, stylish restaurant located just behind Oxford Street.

✚ F4 ✉ 22 St. Christopher's Place, W1 ☎ 020 7486 0777 ⏲ Daily 12–3, 6–11 🚇 Bond Street

CHRISTOPHER'S ££

www.christophersgrill.com

One of the best places in London for a genuine American brunch, Christopher's is in a beautiful Victorian town house with a Martini Bar on the ground floor.

VEGETARIAN EATING

Vegetarians are well-catered to in London. Most restaurants offer a range of meat-free meals, while Indian cooking is famed for its imaginative vegetable and pulse dishes. If fish remains an option, the capital has a wide range on offer.

K5 18 Wellington Street, WC2 020 7240 4222 Mon–Wed 11.30am–midnight, Thu–Sat 11.30am–1.30am, Sun 11.30–10.30 Covent Garden

CLUB GASCON £££

www.clubgascon.com

Good for that special dinner, Club Gascon serves unusual, robust dishes from Gascony. Reserve well in advance.

N3 57 West Smithfield, EC1 020 7600 6144 Mon–Fri 12–2, 6.30–10, Sat 6.30–10.30 Barbican, Farringdon

THE DOG AND DUCK £

www.nicholsonspubs.co.uk/thedogandducksoholondon

Quality beers, cask ales and hearty classic British pub food feature in this pub that's full of character and boasts of serving John Constable, George Orwell and Madonna.

J4 18 Bateman Street, W1 020 7494 0697 Daily 10am–11pm, food served 10–10 Tottenham Court Road

FIFTEEN ££

www.fifteen.net

At Fifteen, popular TV chef Jamie Oliver takes inspiration from around the world for his rustic yet elegant dishes, using the best of British ingredients on the daily changing menu. The cocktail bar has tempting snacks.

Q1 15 Westland Place, N1 020 3375 1515 Mon–Sat 12–3, 6–11, Sun 12–3, 6–10 Old Street

FOOD FOR THOUGHT £

http://foodforthought-london.co.uk

This basement Covent Garden stalwart has been pleasing vegetarians for decades. It's tiny, cramped and you may have to share a table, but that's part of the charm, as are the big servings and low prices.

K4 31 Neal Street, WC2 020 7836 0239 Mon–Sat 12–8, Sun 12–5 Covent Garden

A classic club sandwich

Modern British cuisine uses the finest ingredients

GABY'S DELI £

Inspired by a New York Jewish diner, this is the place to head for no-nonsense food, either to eat in or take out. The falafels are good.

J5 30 Charing Cross Road, WC2 020 7836 4233 Mon–Sat 12–midnight, Sun 12–11 Leicester Square

GAUCHO £££

www.gauchorestaurants.co.uk

Meat-eaters will relish the steaks at this Argentinian restaurant and wine bar. Or, for a lighter meal, try the tasty *ceviches* (marinated raw fish). Excellent South American wines complement the food. The top floor has live music.

H5 25 Swallow Street, W1 020 7734 4040 Mon–Sat 12–midnight, Sun 12–11 Piccadilly Circus

LE GAVROCHE £££

www.le-gavroche.co.uk

Albert's Roux's son sticks to classic French cuisine, but creates lighter dishes. Enjoy amazing wines and a grand setting.

E5 43 Upper Brook Street, W1 020 7408 0881 Mon–Fri 12–2, 6–10, Sat 6–10 Marble Arch

THE GLASSHOUSE £££

www.glasshouserestaurant.co.uk

The perfect preamble to a walk in Kew Gardens or for a special evening out, the Glasshouse serves notable modern dishes, beautifully presented. The owners are passionate about wine, too, so the list is impressive. Reserve in advance.

Off map 14 Station Parade, Kew 020 8940 6777 Mon–Sat 12–2.30, 6.30–10.30, Sun 12.30–3, 7–10 Kew Gardens

GREENHOUSE £££

www.greenhouserestaurant.co.uk

Chef Arnaud Bignon serves imaginative yet serious food, complemented by superb wines. Choose from the à la carte, seasonal, lunch or tasting menus.

G6 27a Hay's Mews, W1 020 7499 3331 Mon–Fri 12–2.30, 6.30–10.30, Sat 6.30–10.30 Green Park

THE GUN ££

www.thegundocklands.com

A popular, comfortable gastropub on Canary Wharf, with stunning views, The Gun serves imaginative, seasonal British food. A typical choice from the menu would be the Brixham plaice.

Off map 27 Coldharbour, Isle of Dogs, E14 020 7515 5222 Mon–Sat 11am–midnight, Sun 11–11 Canary Wharf, Blackwall

HIBISCUS £££

www.hibiscusrestaurant.co.uk

Chef Claude Bosi's bold, inventive, modern French cooking never fails to get rave reviews.

G5 29 Maddox Street, W1S 020 7629 2999 Tue–Thu 12–2.30, 6.30–10.30, Fri–Sat 12–2.30, 6–10.30 Oxford Circus

THE BILL

When the bill (check) arrives, read it carefully. A 12.5 percent service charge, or more, may have been added. If the service you received has not been satisfactory, or if you prefer to tip your waiter in cash, ask them to remove it. A hefty bill can quickly mount up so, to avoid any unpleasant surprises, check whether VAT and coffee are included and if there's a cover charge. Order tap water if you don't want to pay for bottled water.

The unmistakable OXO Tower

ICEBAR LONDON £–££

www.icebarlondon.com

Sip a cocktail in London's "coolest" bar, created from Swedish ice.

H5 H31–33 Heddon Street, W1 020 7478 8910 Mon–Wed 3.30–11, Thu 2.45–11, Fri 2pm–12.30am, Sat 11.45am–12.30am, Sun 2–11 Oxford Circus, Piccadilly Circus

INN THE PARK £

www.peytonandbyrne.co.uk/inn-the-park

Enjoy inspired British food with lake and park views. Afternoon tea is served daily 3–4.30pm.

J7 St. James's Park, SW1 020 7451 9999 Daily 8–11 (9–11 Sat–Sun), 12–5 St. James's Park

JOE ALLEN ££

www.joeallen.co.uk

For American food and beer head to this dependably convivial and clublike establishment. Reservations are essential.

K5 13 Exeter Street, WC2 020 7836 0651 Mon–Thu 12–midnight, Sat 11am–1am, Sun 11am–midnight Covent Garden

LOWLANDER GRAND CAFÉ £

www.lowlander.com

This Belgian bar and brasserie is in a great spot for a pre-theater meal. Try the rib-eye *steak frites*.

K4 36 Drury Lane, WC2 020 7379 7446 Mon–Wed 10–10, Thu 10–11, Fri–Sat 9am–midnight, Sun 9am–10.30pm Covent Garden

MAGGIE JONES'S ££

www.maggie-jones.co.uk

This cosy Kensington institution has been around for over 40 years and is much-loved for its informality, wine list and no-nonsense British food.

Off map 6 Old Court Place, Kensington Church Street, W8 020 7937 6462 Daily 12–2.30, 6–11 (Sun 10) High Street Kensington

MASALA ZONE ££

www.masalazone.com

From the creators of Chutney Mary and Veeraswamy, both known for their authentic dishes, comes an informal setting for *thalis* and Indian street food. There are other branches in the capital.

H5 9 Marshall Street, W1 020 7287 9966 Mon–Sat 12–11, Sun 12.30–10.30 Oxford Circus

SET-PRICE MENUS

Many of London's pricier restaurants offer two set-price menus—lower in price at lunchtime. Try classic Anglo-French cuisine at the Connaught Grill (E5 16 Carlos Place, W1 020 7107 8880) or lunch at Gordon Ramsey's Maze (▷ 149). Most of the star chefs offer these menus, including Tom Aikins, Richard Corrigan and Philip Howard.

MAZE ££–£££

www.gordonramsay.com/maze

Enjoy Gordon Ramsay's truly imaginative haute cuisine—French with Asian influences—in a congenial atmosphere. The three- and four-course lunchtime set menus are competitively priced.

F5 10–13 Grosvenor Square, W1 020 7107 0000 Daily 12–3, 6–11 Bond Street

MEDCALF £–££

www.medcalfbar.co.uk

The carefully crafted British menu changes daily and respects top-quality ingredients.

M2 40 Exmouth Market, EC1 020 7833 3533 Mon–Fri 12–3, 5.30–10.30, Sat 9.30–3, 5.30–10.30, Sun 9.30–5.30; Bar: Sun 12–5.30 Farringdon

THE ORANGERY £

www.hrp.org.uk

A fine 18th-century building overlooking Kensington Palace's formal gardens creates the perfect setting for elegant light lunches or afternoon tea—cucumber sandwiches and scones with jam and cream.

A6 Kensington Palace, Kensington Gardens, W8 020 3166 6113 Mar–Oct daily 10–6; Nov–Feb 10–5 High Street Kensington

OTTOLENGHI £

www.ottolenghi.co.uk

Merely looking at the restaurant is sustaining; eating here around the communal tables is even better. The Mediterranean-influenced dishes are fresh, colorful and full of flavor. Favorites include roast chicken with chilli and basil and roasted sweet potato with pecan and maple syrup. The restaurant is opposite the Almeida Theatre.

INDIAN FOOD

London's 2,000 or so Indian restaurants cater to a well-informed local clientele. An Indian meal should have many dishes so, if you are a group, consider making a collective order and sharing. Tandoori dishes (cooked in a clay oven) make good starters. A North Indian meal's main course might include one or two meat offerings, two or three vegetable dishes, rice, a lentil or other pulse, and a variety of breads such as chapatti or naan—which are eaten hot, so order more as you go along. Remember the yogurt and pickles, and drink *lassi* (sweet or salty variations on buttermilk/yogurt) or beer.

Off map 287 Upper Street, N1 020 7288 1454 Mon–Sat 8am–10.30pm, Sun 9am–7pm Angel, Highbury & Islington

OXO TOWER BAR, BRASSERIE AND RESTAURANT ££–£££

www.harveynichols.com

Look out over London while eating, drinking or snacking on vibrantly modern British and pan-Asian food. There are plenty of outdoor tables but reservations are essential.

M6 8th Floor, Oxo Tower Wharf, Barge House Street, SE1 020 7803 3888 Mon–Sat 12–11, Sun 12–10, Blackfriars

PAUL £

www.paul-uk.com

This patisserie is a branch of its French mother founded in 1889. Sample divine hot chocolate and pastries. There are more than 30 other branches across London.

K5 29 Bedford Street, WC2 020 7836 3304 Mon–Fri 7am–9pm, Sat–Sun 8am–9pm Covent Garden

BUFFET DEALS

Unlimited food at a fixed price is practical for families with growing children—or simply for hungry adults. Many larger hotels do breakfast and lunch buffets, especially good on Sunday when many Indian restaurants do the same.

THE PEASANT £–££

www.thepeasant.co.uk

Expect a warm welcome at this north London gastropub. Classic and modern British food is served in the bar, with more sophisticated flavors on offer in the upstairs restaurant.

N3 240 St. John Street, EC1 020 7336 7726 Mon–Sat 12–11, Sun 12–10.30 Farringdon

PORTRAIT RESTAURANT ££

www.npg.org.uk

Up on level three of the National Portrait Gallery, every table here has a fine view. Try the salmon with cream sauce for a summer lunch. Reservations are essential.

J5 National Portrait Gallery, St. Martin's Place, WC2 020 7312 2490 Daily 10–11, 11.45–2.45, 3.30–4.45; Thu– Sat 5.30–8.15 Leicester Square, Charing Cross

LA POULE AU POT ££

www.pouleaupot.co.uk

A Belgravia institution, loved as much for its romantic, retro country atmosphere as its classic French cooking. Think bouillabaisse, boeuf bourgignon, cassoulet and tarte tatin. In summer, the outdoor terrace is popular for alfresco trysts.

Off map at F9 231 Ebury Street, SW1 020 7730 7763 Mon–Fri 12–2.30, 6.45–11, Sat 12–4, 6.45–11, Sun 12–4, 6.45–10 Sloane Square

PROVIDORES & TAPA ROOM ££

www.theprovidores.co.uk

Enjoy imaginative dishes and New Zealand wines at this café, wine bar and fine dining restaurant.

F3 109 Marylebone High Street, W1 020 7935 6175 Mon–Sat 9am–10.30pm, Sun 9–10 Baker Street

RASA W1 £

www.rasarestaurants.com

One of several Rasa restaurants in the capital, Rasa W1 serves inspired cooking from Kerala in southwest India, with seafood and vegetarian dishes as specialties.

H3 6 Dering Street, W1 020 7629 1346 Mon–Sat 12–3, 6–11, Sun 1–8 Oxford Circus, Bond Street

RESTAURANT AT ST PAUL'S £

www.restaurantatstpauls.co.uk

Serving good food at sensible prices in pleasing surroundings beneath Wren's Cathedral (▷ 44), this is a gem in this part of town.

N4 St Paul's Churchyard, EC4 020 7248 2469 Lunch: daily 12–3; afternoon tea: Mon–Sat 3–4.15 St Paul's

ROYAL CHINA £–££

http://rcguk.co.uk

Reserve a table or join the justifiably long lines for the best dim sum in town, served from 12–4.45.

A5 13 Queensway, W2 020 7221 2535 Mon–Sat 12–11, Sun 11–10 Queensway

RULES ££

www.rules.co.uk

Rules, founded in 1798, serves good traditional English dishes in plush Edwardian rooms.

K5 35 Maiden Lane, WC2 020 7836 5314 Mon–Sat 12–11.45, Sun 12–10.45 Covent Garden

ST. JOHN ££
www.stjohngroup.uk.com
The robust dishes on offer range from rabbit to oxtail to serious puddings, such as lemon posset.
N3 26 St. John Street, EC1 020 7521 0848 Mon–Fri 12–3, Mon–Sat 6pm–11pm, Sun 1–3 Farringdon

THE SQUARE £££
www.squarerestaurant.com
Impressive modern French food from Philip Howard is matched by a chic but formal Mayfair interior.
G5 6–10 Bruton Street, W1 020 7495 7100 Mon–Sat 12–2.45, 6.30–10 (Fri–Sat 10.30), Sun 6.30–9.30 Bond Street, Green Park

TAMARIND ££
www.tamarindrestaurant.com
Focusing on traditional Mughal cuisine, cooked in tandoor ovens and delicately spiced, Alfred Prassad won the UK's first Michelin star for an Indian restaurant.
G6 20 Queen Street, W1 020 7629 3561 Mon–Fri 12–2.45, 5.30–11, Sat 5.30–11, Sun 12–2.45, 6–10.30 Green Park

TATE MODERN CAFÉ £
www.tate.org.uk
Take a break from the art to enjoy upscale café food and Thames views. For a grander meal, book at the rooftop restaurant.
N6 Tate Modern, SE1 020 7401 5014 Mon–Thu 10–5.30, Fri 10–8.30, Sat 10–6.30, Sun 10–6 Blackfriars, Southwark

TOM'S KITCHEN £–££
This is a vibrant, modern British restaurant, deli and summer terrace bar set in the splendour of Somerset House (▷ 50).
L5 Somerset House, Strand, WC2 020 7845 4646 Lunch Mon–Fri 12–3; Dinner Mon–Sat 6–10, brunch Sat–Sun 10–4; Deli Mon–Fri 8–6, Sat–Sun 10–6 Blackfriars

VILLANDRY ££
www.villandry.com
Villandry delights with its simple but tasty specialties. There's a French delicatessen, bakery, café and bar, too.
G3 170 Great Portland Street, W1 020 7631 3131 Mon–Fri 7.30am–10.30pm, Sat 8am–10.30pm, Sun 9–6 Great Portland Street, Regents Park

WILD FOOD CAFÉ £
www.wildfoodcafe.com
This cafe is dedicated to making you feel great, with a host of raw and plant-based dishes (whole-food, vegan and vegetarian).
K4 1st floor, 14 Neal's Yard, WC2 020 7419 2014 Sun–Mon 12–5, Tue–Sat 12–10 Covent Garden

WILD HONEY ££–£££
www.wildhoneyrestaurant.co.uk
Enjoy quality modern European cooking in a stylishly simple Mayfair setting. The set lunch and pre-theater menus are good value.
G5 12 St. George Street, W1 020 7758 9160 Mon–Sat 12–2.30, 6–11 Oxford Circus, Bond Street

THE WOLSELEY ££
www.thewolseley.com
The Grand Café tradition continues at the Wolseley in Piccadilly. Start the day in art deco grandeur, or relax over afternoon tea after visiting the Royal Academy.
H6 160 Piccadilly, W1 020 7499 6996 Mon–Fri 7am–midnight, Sat 8am–midnight, Sun 8am–11pm Green Park, Piccadilly Circus

7494

Sleep

With options ranging from the luxurious to simple budget hotels, London has accommodations to suit everyone. In this section establishments are listed alphabetically.

Introduction	**154**
Directory	**155**
Sleeping A–Z	**155**

Introduction

London has many excellent hotels but room rates are very high, and it is certainly worth searching for special offers. Weekend and winter rates are often less expensive.

Reservations

Many hotels will ask you to pre-pay your reservation, or confirm with a credit card, and will charge a fee if you cancel at short notice or fail to turn up. Most hotels have rooms of different sizes, so always ask if there is a choice. Small hotels and guesthouses in historic buildings may not have a lift (elevator).

Outside Central London

If you are prepared to take a slightly longer bus or Tube ride to reach the sights, staying in a residential suburb provides a less expensive alternative to a pricey city-center hotel.

Budget Accommodations

Consider alternatives to hotels, such as renting an apartment, staying in a bed-and-breakfast (B&B) or staying with a London family (for online information visit www.bedandbreakfast.com, www.athomeinlondon.co.uk or the tourist board's www.visitlondon.com). During student vacations, inexpensive accommodations are offered by London university halls of residence (see www.universityrooms.co.uk and www.ish.org.uk). Youth hostels are another inexpensive option (www.yha.org.uk).

NOISE LEVELS

As most of London's accommodation options are situated on busy streets, noise can be a problem. Some hotels have double glazing, but that can make rooms unbearably stuffy, especially since air-conditioning is not standard. If you value peace and quiet, look for hotels on side streets in residential areas or request a room at the rear or higher up in the building.

Top to bottom: The exclusive Claridge's Hotel; the grand entrance to The Dorchester; London's top hotels offer superb service; a room at the Grosvenor Hotel

Directory

South Bank

Budget
Premier Inn
Southwark Rose

Fleet Street to the Tower

Budget
Travelodge
Mid-Range
Chamberlain
Zetter Rooms
Luxury
Andaz
Malmaison
The Rookery

Covent Garden to Regent's Park

Budget
Morgan
Mid-Range
Academy
Luxury
Charlotte Street Hotel
Covent Garden Hotel
Hazlitt's
One Aldwych
St. Martin's Lane
Savoy

Westminster and St. James's

Luxury
The Goring
The Ritz

Around Hyde Park

Budget
22 York Street
Easyhotel
Pavilion Hotel
Mid-Range
Aster House
Kensington House
The Leonard
Luxury
The Berkeley
Blakes
The Dorchester
The Halkin

Farther Afield

Mid-Range
The Beaver
Henley House Portobello

Sleeping A–Z

PRICES

Prices are approximate and based on a double room for one night.

£££	Over £250
££	£150–£250
£	under £150

22 YORK STREET £

www.22yorkstreet.co.uk
This elegant five-story Georgian town house close to Regent's Park has been transformed into a quality bed-and-breakfast.
E3 22 York Street, W1 020 7224 2990 Baker Street

ACADEMY ££

www.theetoncollection.co.uk
Convenient for the British Museum, this 49-room boutique hotel is set in five converted Georgian town houses.
J3 21 Gower Street, WC1 020 7631 4115 Goodge Street

ANDAZ £££

www.london.liverpoolstreet.andaz.hyatt.co.uk

Casual 21st-century luxury is the theme of this stylishly converted Victorian railway hotel.

R3 40 Liverpool Street, EC2 020 7961 1234 Liverpool Street

ASTER HOUSE ££

www.asterhouse.com

Aster House stands with other chic B&Bs in a smart South Kensington stuccoed terrace, near the museums. You can enjoy the garden, palm-filled conservatory and power showers.

C9 3 Sumner Place, SW7 020 7581 5888 South Kensington

THE BEAVER £

www.beaverhotel.co.uk

Bed-and-breakfast accommodation on a tree-lined Victorian crescent, conveniently located for transport and South Kensington's museums.

Off map at A9 57–59 Philbeach Gardens, SW5 020 7373 4553 Earl's Court

THE BERKELEY £££

www.the-berkeley.co.uk

Guests at this luxury Knightsbridge hotel enjoy traditional elegance, plus famed service and food.

LOCATION

It is well worth perusing the London map to decide where you are likely to spend most of your time. Then select a hotel in that area or accessible to it by Underground on a direct line, so you avoid having to change trains. London is vast and it takes time to cross, particularly by bus and costly taxis. By paying a little more to be in the heart of the city, you will save on travel time and costs.

Facilities include a spa, rooftop pool and two great restaurants.

E7 Wilton Place, SW1 020 7235 6000 Hyde Park Corner, Knightsbridge

BLAKES ££–£££

www.blakeshotels.com

Designer Anoushka Hempel has achieved sumptuous decadence in this South Kensington boutique hotel. There are just 41 rooms, plus a restaurant and bar.

Off map 33 Roland Gardens, SW7 020 7370 6701 South Kensington, Gloucester Road

CHAMBERLAIN ££

www.thechamberlainhotel.co.uk

In lavishly converted 20th-century offices in the City of London, this hotel has 64 comfortable bedrooms. There is a popular pub on the premises.

S4 130–135 Minories, EC3 020 7680 1500 Fenchurch Street, Aldgate

CHARLOTTE STREET HOTEL £££

www.firmdalehotels.com

Kit and Tim Kemp's boutique cocktail of comfort and fairy-tale Englishness has 52 rooms.

H3 15 Charlotte Street, W1 020 7806 2000 Goodge Street

COVENT GARDEN HOTEL £££

www.firmdalehotels.com

Another of Kit Kemp's stylish boutique hotels, this one attracts film stars who enjoy its 58 traditional yet contemporary British rooms, bathrooms and library.

J4 10 Monmouth Street, WC2 020 7806 1000 Leicester Square

THE DORCHESTER £££

www.thedorchester.com

The Dorchester is one of London's

finest hotels. Deliciously art deco, it is a London landmark from its grand entrance and piano bar to the Oliver Messel suite. The hotel's 250 bedrooms have huge, luxury bathrooms.
F6 Park Lane, W1 020 7629 8888 Green Park, Hyde Park Corner

EASYHOTEL £

www.easyhotel.com

Easyhotel is inexpensive but basic in the extreme; few of the 34 rooms have windows.
A8 14 Lexham Gardens, W8 Reserve by website only Earl's Court, Gloucester Road

THE GORING £££

www.thegoring.com

High standards of old-fashioned hospitality and service make this splendid hotel, with its 74 luxurious and classic rooms, memorable. It's where the Middleton family stayed before Kate's wedding to Prince William.
G8 Beeston Place, Grosvenor Gardens, SW1 020 7396 9000 Victoria

HIDDEN COSTS

The room price quoted by a hotel may, or may not, include Continental or full English breakfast and VAT, which is currently 20 percent. Since these affect the bill dramatically, it is vital to ask in advance what is included in the price. Also check the percentage markup on telephone and internet connection and business office facilities, and ask about the laundry service, which can be very slow.

THE HALKIN £££

www.comohotels.com/thehalkin

With a stylish blend of Western and Asian aesthetics, this 41-room boutique hotel has a Michelin-starred Basque restaurant.
F7 4 Halkin Street, SW1 020 7333 1000 Hyde Park Corner

HAZLITT'S £££

www.hazlittshotel.com

The 23-room Hazlitt's has near-perfect period decoration in three 18th-century houses, plus it's in a superb location for Theatreland.
J4 6 Frith Street, W1 020 7434 1771 Tottenham Court Road

The Dorchester, one of the capital's finest hotels

MODERN HOTELS

London has many contemporary hotels, from starkly minimal to sumptuously luxurious. At the top end, try the Andaz Hotel (▷ 156), Kit Kemp's six London hotels (www.firmdalehotels.com), Sanderson (✉ 50 Berners Street, W1 ☎ 020 7300 1400, www.sandersonlondon.com), No. 5 Maddox Street (✉ 5 Maddox Street, W1 ☎ 020 7647 0200, www.living-rooms.co.uk) or myhotel Bloomsbury (✉ 11–13 Bayley Street, Bedford Square, WC1 ☎ 020 3004 6000, www.myhotels.co.uk) near the British Museum.

The Savoy, a byword for luxury

HENLEY HOUSE £–££

www.henleyhousehotel.com

A small guesthouse with 21 recently upgraded rooms overlooking a garden square and close to good transport options.

✚ Off map at A9 ✉ 30 Barkston Gardens, SW5 ☎ 020 7370 4111 🚇 Earl's Court

KENSINGTON HOUSE ££

www.kenhouse.com

This beautifully restored 19th-century property provides contemporary accommodations in the heart of Kensington. The 41 bedrooms are light and stylish.

✚ A7 ✉ 15–16 Prince of Wales Terrace, W8 ☎ 020 7937 2345 🚇 High Street Kensington

THE LEONARD ££–£££

www.theleonard.com

A discreet, small hotel, near busy Oxford Street, the Leonard has 48 comfortable bedrooms and luxury apartments.

✚ E4 ✉ 15 Seymour Street, W1 ☎ 020 7935 2010 🚇 Marble Arch

MALMAISON £££

www.malmaison.com

Relax in the stylish, contemporary rooms at this hotel with a brasserie and bar in trendy Clerkenwell.

✚ N3 ✉ 18 Charterhouse Square, EC1 🚇 Farringdon

MORGAN £

www.morganhotel.co.uk

Family-run, friendly and well-located, the Morgan has just 20 rooms, so book ahead.

✚ J3 ✉ 24 Bloomsbury Street, WC1 ☎ 020 7636 3735 🚇 Tottenham Court Road

ONE ALDWYCH £££

www.onealdwych.com

A stylish, 105-room contemporary hotel in an Edwardian building, One Aldwych epitomizes restrained luxury.

✚ L5 ✉ 1 Aldwych, WC2 ☎ 020 7300 1000 🚇 Covent Garden, Temple

PAVILION HOTEL £

www.pavilionhoteluk.com

The plain facade at the 30-room Pavilion Hotel belies the witty fantasy decor inside.

✚ C4 ✉ 34–36 Sussex Gardens, W2 ☎ 020 7262 0905 🚇 Paddington

PORTOBELLO ££

www.portobello-hotel.co.uk

A romantic retreat with 24 exotic, sumptuous rooms, the hotel is

within easy reach of the antiques shops of Portobello Road.
Off map 22 Stanley Gardens, W11 020 7727 2777 Notting Hill Gate

PREMIER INN £
www.premierinn.com
In County Hall, opposite the Houses of Parliament, this 313-room hotel is the star London location of the no-frills chain.
L7 County Hall, Belvedere Road, SE1 Waterloo

THE RITZ £££
www.theritzlondon.com
Guests enjoy sumptuous luxury, with traditional style, gilt decor and the great first-floor promenade to London's most beautiful dining room, overlooking Green Park.
G6 150 Piccadilly, W1 020 7493 8181 Green Park

THE ROOKERY £££
www.rookeryhotel.co.uk
Enjoy discreet comforts in this atmospheric 33-room hotel, enhanced with antiques, open fires and Victorian bathrooms.
N3 12 Peter's Lane, Cowcross Street, EC1 020 7336 0931 Farringdon

ST. MARTIN'S LANE £££
www.stmartinslane.com
Ian Schrager and Philippe Starck's fabulous 204-room hotel in Covent Garden is a celebration of theatrical minimalism.
J5 45 St. Martin's Lane, WC2 020 7300 5500 Covent Garden, Leicester Square

SAVOY £££
www.fairmont.com/savoy-london
A top-to-toe refurbishment has brought this grand London hotel firmly into the 21st century. It has a perfect spot next to the Thames.
L5 Strand, WC2 020 7836 4343 Covent Garden

SOUTHWARK ROSE £
www.ibis.com
This Ibis Styles hotel with 114 rooms is close to Tate Modern and, via the Millennium Bridge, the rest of the city center.
P6 43–47 Southwark Bridge Road, SE1 020 7015 1480 London Bridge

TRAVELODGE £
www.travelodge.co.uk
Part of the no-frills budget chain, this London Central Tower Bridge Travelodge is a good choice.
S5 1 Goodmans Yard, Lloyds Court Business Centre, E1 Tower Hill

ZETTER ROOMS ££
www.thezetter.com
A cool hotel in Clerkenwell, with a restaurant and bar to match, the Zetter has 59 rooms. The rooms are decorated in a modern vintage style. There are great views of the City from the rooftop suites.
N2 St. John's Square, 86–88 Clerkenwell Road, EC1 020 7324 4444 Farringdon

BARGAIN LUXURY

To be pampered amid sumptuous surroundings may be an essential part of your trip. London's most luxurious hotels have been built with no expense spared. Hotel prices are generally very high, but quality rooms can be had for a discounted price. It's always worth asking when you make your reservation whether any special deals are available. Most deluxe and mid-range hotels offer weekend deals throughout the year.

THAMES PATH
IMPERIAL WAR MUSEUM
LONDON AQUARIUM
THAMES PATH
Hungerford Bridge
ST. THOMAS'S HOSPI
(Florence Nightingale Mu
WHITEHALL
EMBANKMENT
WESTMINSTER

Need to Know

This section takes you through all the practical aspects of your trip to make it run more smoothly and to give you confidence before you go and while you are there.

Planning Ahead	**162**
Getting There	**164**
Getting Around	**166**
Essential Facts	**168**
Books and Films	**171**

Planning Ahead

WHEN TO GO

London is busy year-round, and most attractions remain open all year. Peak season is from May to September, when you should arrive with a hotel reservation and theater tickets. The quietest months are January to March and November, when hotels may give a discount.

TIME

GMT (Greenwich Mean Time) is standard. BST (British Summer Time) is 1 hour ahead (late Mar–late Oct).

TEMPERATURE

JAN	FEB	MAR	APR	MAY	JUN	JUL	AUG	SEP	OCT	NOV	DEC
42°F	45°F	50°F	55°F	63°F	68°F	72°F	72°F	66°F	57°F	50°F	45°F
6°C	7°C	10°C	13°C	17°C	20°C	22°C	22°C	19°C	14°C	10°C	7°C

Spring (March to May) has a mixture of sunshine and showers, although winter often encroaches on it.

Summer (June to August) can be unpredictable, with clear skies and hot days interspersed with rain, sultry grayness or thunderstorms.

Autumn (September to November) often has clear skies that can feel almost summery. Real autumn starts in October, and colder weather sets in during November.

Winter (December to February) is generally fairly cold, and snow has been disruptive in recent years.

WHAT'S ON

January *Sales:* Shopping bargains at stores all over the city.

February *Chinese New Year:* Dragon dances and fireworks in Chinatown.

March *Chelsea Antiques Fair:* Treasures at Chelsea Old Town Hall.

April *Oxford and Cambridge Boat Race* (1st Sat): This famous annual race takes place on the Thames from Putney to Mortlake.

London Marathon: 40,000 runners zigzag through the capital.

May *Chelsea Flower Show* (end of May): One of the world's best shows takes place at the Royal Hospital, Chelsea.

June *Trooping the Colour* (2nd Sat): The "Colours" (flags) are trooped before the Queen on Horseguards Parade, Whitehall.

Wimbledon (Jun/Jul): The world's leading grass tennis tournament.

July *Promenade Concerts* (Jul–Aug): Nightly world-class classical concerts in the Albert Hall.

August *Notting Hill Carnival* (last Sun and Bank Holiday Monday): Europe's biggest carnival.

September *Totally Thames Festival* (all month): Arts, culture and river events along the 42-mile stretch of the Thames in London.

October *The Big Draw*: The world's largest celebration of drawing.

BFI London Film Festival.

November *Bonfire Night* (5 Nov): Fires and fireworks commemorate the failed Gunpowder Plot of 1605.

Lord Mayor's Show: The City of London's favorite ritual, with parades and pageantry in a long procession.

December *Christmas music* (all month): Christmas music fills London's churches and many concert halls.

LONDON ONLINE

www.visitlondon.com
London's official site is up-to-date and comprehensive with ideas for museums, theater and restaurants, and sections for children and visitors with disabilities. It offers discounts, too.

www.royalparks.org.uk
From Greenwich Park to Green Park, all eight of London's Royal Parks are detailed here, with information on special events and activities for children.

www.tfl.gov.uk
London Transport's official site gives ideas for what to see and do, ticket information for the Underground, buses, DLR and river services. It also has a WAP-enabled journey planner.

www.royal.gov.uk
The official site of the British royal family, with history, royal residences, who's doing what today and a monthly online magazine.

www.bhrconline.com
The British Hotel Reservation Centre website takes bookings, from bed-and-breakfasts to grand hotels. Special discounts are included.

www.londontown.com
This comprehensive site covers what's on, what's new, attractions, events, theaters, sightseeing ideas, traditions, nightlife, shopping, markets and general advice.

www.hrp.org.uk
This site is dedicated to London's five great historic palaces, from the Tower of London to Hampton Court Palace.

www.officiallondontheatre.co.uk
The Society of London Theatre's official site, with all the latest theater news, together with comprehensive interviews with stars, performance details and theater access for visitors with disabilities.

TRAVEL SITES

www.nationaltrust.org.uk
This independent organization owns and maintains many buildings and extensive lands, some of them in and around London.

www.english-heritage.org.uk/London
English Heritage is responsible for many historic sites and buildings—with ideas for days out in London.

www.fodors.com
A complete travel-planning site. You can research prices and weather, book air tickets, cars and rooms, pose questions (and get answers) from fellow travelers, and find links to other sites.

www.visitbritain.com
Great places to visit around the UK, with accommodation, transport, special offers and travel tips.

INTERNET ACCESS

All of the capital's public libraries have internet facilities. WiFi is available at Starbucks and Costa cafés, major train stations and airports. Most hotels have modem plug-in-points (data ports) or WiFi in each room.

Getting There

TRAINS

- For all information, visit National Rail at www.nationalrail.co.uk
- Purchase tickets at the railway station or on online at www.thetrainline.com.
- All major London train stations are on Tube lines.
- There are eight major London train stations and sometimes a town is served by more than one (e.g. Paddington and Waterloo both serve Windsor).
- Train fares are high but there are lots of cheap deals if you book in advance and can be flexible about the time you travel.

NIGHT BUS

At night the N9 bus connects Heathrow with central London (Trafalgar Square) about every 20 minutes from the central bus station.

AIRPORTS

Heathrow and Gatwick are the principal airports serving the city. However, Stansted, Luton and London City are becoming increasingly busy with traffic from Continental Europe. There are train links to the continent via Lille and Paris and road links to Channel ports.

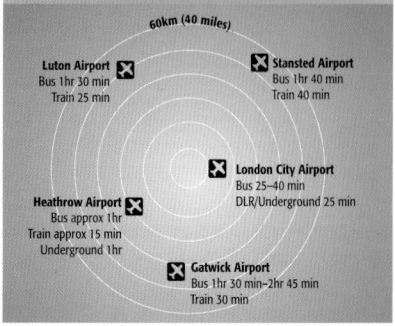

FROM HEATHROW

Heathrow (www.heathrowairport.com) has five terminals, 32km (20 miles) west of central London; all are well served by public transport. The Tube's Piccadilly line runs from 5am to 11.40pm (Heathrow Terminal 4 station closes Mon–Sat 11.35pm, Sun 11.15pm) and takes about an hour. The Heathrow Express (www.heathrowexpress.com), a high-speed rail link to Paddington station, runs from 5.10am to 11.40pm every 15 minutes. Prices are high for the 15-minute journey. Try the Heathrow Connect service (www.heathrowconnect.com) to Paddington station. Two trains an hour operate on this stopping service. The journey time is around 25 minutes and the cost is less than half than that of the express fares.

National Express (www.nationalexpress.com) coaches run from 8.55am to 9pm to Victoria Coach Station, journey time around 1 hour 40 minutes. Taxis wait outside the terminals; the trip takes under an hour, depending on traffic, and costs from £50 to £70.

FROM GATWICK

Gatwick airport (www.gatwickairport.com) is 48km (30 miles) south of the heart of the city.

The best way to reach London is by train. The Gatwick Express (www.gatwickexpress. com) train leaves for Victoria Station every 15 minutes, (4.35am–12.50am) and takes 30 minutes. Southern runs slightly slower but cheaper services and Govia Thameslink (www.thameslinkrailway.com) go direct to the City and King's Cross/St. Pancras International. Taxis cost more than £100.

FROM STANSTED

Stansted airport (www.stanstedairport.com) is 56km (35 miles) northeast of central London. The Stansted Express (www.stanstedexpress. com) to Liverpool Street Station takes around 50 minutes. Several bus/coach operators run services to Liverpool Street and Victoria stations. Journey time is up to 1 hour 40 minutes. A taxi costs from £100.

FROM LUTON AIRPORT

Luton airport (www.london-luton.co.uk) is 53km (33 miles) north of London. There are bus links to Victoria Coach Station, taking around 1 hour 30 minutes, and East Midlands and Thameslink trains to St. Pancras International, taking from 25 minutes. Taxis cost about £80.

FROM LONDON CITY AIRPORT

City Airport (www.londoncityairport.com) is at Royal Albert Docks, 14km (9 miles) east of central London. Trains from London City Airport DLR station feed into the Underground system. Taxis from the terminal cost around £35.

THE CHANNEL TUNNEL

Eurostar train services (www.eurostar.com) connect Britain to Continental Europe, and are a great way of arriving in London, plus taking trips out to Paris, Brussels and elsewhere in Europe. The journey to Brussels takes about 2 hours, Paris about 2 hours 15 mins. Trains depart from St. Pancras International terminal, close to King's Cross. Eurotunnel (www.eurotunnel.com) is for vehicles only. Fares are lower if you reserve ahead.

BY COACH

If you travel to London by long-distance coach you will probably arrive at Victoria Coach Station (VCS) on Buckingham Palace Road, near Victoria main train station. The coach station is a few minutes' walk from the Underground station, which is on the Victoria, District and Circle lines. Alternatively, there is a taxi rank immediately outside VCS.

LOST/STOLEN PROPERTY

Even the most seasoned traveler occasionally leaves something behind—airlines find forgotten computers almost daily.

- Contact the place where you think you left it or saw it last.
- Report the loss to a police station and get a copy of the report form for your insurance claim.
- If you lose your passport, report it to the police and your embassy immediately. Provided you have photocopies of the key pages, it should not be difficult to replace but there's usually a charge.
- Contact for London Transport and taxi lost property ☎ 0343 222 1234, www.tfl.gov.uk

Getting Around

DRIVING TIP

Driving in London is slow, parking is expensive and fines are high. Congestion charges operate from Monday to Friday, 7am–6pm, costing £11.50 a day. Do not drive in London unless you have to, use public transport instead.

VISITORS WITH DISABILITIES

London is steadily improving its facilities for visitors with disabilities, from shops and theaters to hotels and museums. The government is introducing free admission for those with disabilities. Newer attractions such as Tate Modern and the London Eye are better equipped than ancient buildings such as Westminster Abbey. Check out the London Tourist Board's comprehensive website (www.visitlondon.com) and guide books, such as *Access in London* (published by Access Project PHSP ✉ 39 Bradley Gardens, W13, www.accessinlondon.org). Also consult Artsline (www.artsline.org.uk), Can Be Done (www.canbedone.co.uk) and Dial (www.scope.org.uk/dial). William Forrester, a lecturer and wheelchair user, leads tailor-made tours in the city (☎ 01483 575401).

Underground trains (known as the Tube) and buses run from around 5.30am to just after midnight, when service is via a night bus. The transport system is divided into zones (clearly indicated on transport maps) and you must have a ticket valid for the zone you are in. If you anticipate making more than one journey, buy a Travelcard (▷ 167), which allows unlimited use of the Underground, buses and Docklands Light Railway (DLR) services. Travel information is available on 0343 222 1234 or at www.tfl.gov.uk.

THE UNDERGROUND (TUBE)

Twelve color-coded lines link almost 300 stations. Use a travel pass or buy a ticket from a machine or ticket booth and keep the ticket until the end of the journey. The system includes the Docklands Light Railway (DLR). From the September 2015, a number of lines will operate all night on Fridays and Saturdays.

BUSES

Plan your journey using the latest copy of the Central London bus guide available at London Transport information centers (▷ 167) or at www.tfl.gov.uk. A flat cash fare applies across London. Tickets must be bought from a machine at the bus stop. A bus stop is indicated by a red sign on a metal pole displaying diagrams of each route it serves.

Look out for the new red double-decker buses, combining cutting-edge design and technology with nostalgia for the old Routemaster buses.

TAXIS

Taxis that are available for rental illuminate a yellow "For Hire" sign on the roof. Hold out your hand to hail them beside the road. Drivers of official cabs will know the city well. They are obliged to follow the shortest route unless an alternative is agreed beforehand.

A black cab (now often not black but a bright color) is licensed for up to five passengers. Meter charges increase in the evenings and at

weekends. Be careful using minicabs, as they may have no meter and possibly inadequate insurance. Call a black cab via Radio Taxis (tel 020 7272 0272, www.radiotaxis.co.uk).

TRAVEL INFORMATION CENTERS

These sell travel passes, provide Tube, train and bus route maps and information on cheap tickets, and open daily at the following stations: Heathrow terminals 1, 2 and 3, Gatwick Airport, Liverpool Street, Victoria, Euston, King's Cross and Piccadilly Circus. Transport for London service, tel 0343 222 1234.

TRAVEL PASSES

Travelcards, valid after 9.30am (you must pay a surcharge to use them earlier), for unlimited travel by Tube, railway, Docklands Light Railway and buses, are sold at travel information centers, railway and Tube stations, and some shops. They cover travel for one day or seven days.

Oyster prepay Smartcards are valid for use on the Underground, DLR, bus, Thameslink and some national rail networks. Single fares are much cheaper with Oyster than cash and the cards can be topped up with more credit. Contactless payment cards are also accepted.

LONDON PASS

A pass to more than 60 top attractions, as well as an option to travel on buses, the Tube and trains, which is valid for either one, two, three or six days—multiday passes must be used on consecutive days. It also offers discounts on restaurants and leisure activities. See www.londonpass.com for details.

BOATING AND BIKING

Thames Clippers (www.thamesclippers.com) runs a commuter, leisure and sightseeing service aboard high-speed catamarans.

London Cycling Campaign (www.lcc.org.uk) can advise on all aspects of biking in the capital. Visitors can rent a bicycle from, and return it to, one of the hundreds of Barclays Cycle Hire project docking stations scattered across London (www.tfl.gov.uk).

TIPS

- London is huge. It may take more than an hour to reach your destination, so allow plenty of time—and plan your day to avoid criss-crossing the city.
- Buy a travelcard, which is valid for the transport network. Select the appropriate pass for the areas you will visit. Zones 1 and 2 range is usually adequate; pay a supplement when you go outside it.
- Use common sense when traveling alone at night, but there is no need to be unduly concerned.
- Smoking is banned on all public transport.

FUN TOURS

Below are some ideas for quirkier ways to explore.

- London Walks (☎ 020 7624 3978, www.walks.com).
- Open House Architecture (☎ 020 3006 7008, www.open-city.org.uk).
- By water (▷ 56–57).
- London Duck Tours (☎ 020 7928 3132, www.londonducktours.co.uk).
- Cable car (☎ 0343 222 1234, www.emiratesairline.co.uk). London's newest transport link is the Emirates Air Line. A cable car across the Thames between North Greenwich and the Royal Docks, it offers easy access to the O2 Arena with great views along the way.

Essential Facts

VISAS AND TRAVEL INSURANCE

Check visa and passport requirements before traveling; see www.fco.gov.uk or ukinusa.fco.gov.uk. EU citizens are covered for medical expenses with an EHIC card; insurance to cover illness and theft is still strongly advised. Visitors from outside the EU should purchase adequate travel insurance.

MONEY

The pound sterling is the official currency in the UK. There are bank notes in denominations 5, 10, 20, and 50, and coins in 1, 2, 5, 20 and 50 pence and 1 and 2 pounds.

CREDIT CARDS

- Credit cards are widely accepted. Visa and MasterCard are the most popular, followed by AmericanExpress, Diners Club and JCB. Credit cards can also be used for withdrawing cash from bank ATMs.
- If your credit cards are lost report each one immediately to the credit card company and, if stolen, the police as well. For your credit card company's local 24-hour emergency number, go to www.ukphonebook.com. It's free but you have to register.

ELECTRICITY

- Standard supply is 240V. Motor-driven equipment needs a specific frequency; in the UK it is 50 cycles per second (kHz).

EMERGENCY TELEPHONE NUMBERS

- For police, fire or ambulance, tel 999 from any telephone, free of charge. The call goes directly to the emergency services. Tell the operator which street you are on and the nearest landmark, intersection or house number; stay by the telephone until help arrives.

MEDICAL TREATMENT

- EU nationals and citizens of some other countries with special arrangements (Australia and New Zealand) may be eligible to receive free National Health Service (NHS) medical treatment provided that they are in possession of the correct documentation (an EHIC card for EU visitors).
- All other visitors have to pay.
- If you need an ambulance tel 999 on any telephone, free of charge, or 112 from most mobiles (cellphones).
- NHS hospitals with 24-hour emergency departments include: University College Hospital, 235 Euston Road, NW1, tel 020 7387 9300; St Mary's Hospital, Praed Street, W2, tel 020 7886 6666; St Thomas' Hospital, Westminster Bridge Road, SE1, tel 020 7188 7188
- Private hospitals, with no emergency unit, include the Cromwell Hospital, 162–174 Cromwell Road, SW5, tel 020 7460 5700.
- Dental problems: King's College Hospital, Denmark Hill, SE5, has an Acute Dental Care clinic for treating serious dental problems. Helpdesk tel 020 3299 3052, Mon–Fri 9–4.30.
- Eye specialist: Moorfields Eye Hospital, City Road, EC1, tel 020 7253 3411, Vision Express, 263–265 Oxford Street, W1, tel 020 7409 7880 (includes an opticians and an on-site workshop for glasses and contact lenses).

• For homeopathic pharmacies, practitioners and advice, contact the British Homeopathic Association, tel 01582 408675, www.britishhomeopathic.org.

MEDICINES

• Many drugs cannot be bought over the counter. For an NHS prescription, you pay a modest flat rate; if a private doctor prescribes, you pay the full cost. To claim charges back on insurance, keep receipts.

• Chemists that keep longer hours include: Bliss Chemist, 5 Marble Arch, W1, tel 020 7723 6116, daily 9am–midnight; Boots Midnight Pharmacy, 44–6 Regent Street, Piccadilly Circus, W1, tel 020 7734 6126; Zafash Pharmacy, 233 Old Brompton Road, SW5, tel 020 7373 2798, is open daily 24 hours.

OPENING HOURS

• Major attractions: Seven days a week; some open late certain days of each week.

• Shops: Generally Mon–Sat 9.30/10am–6pm; department stores until 8 or even 10pm (Selfridges, Oxford Street). Many shops open Sun 12–5/6pm; department stores have browsing time before the tills open from 11.30am. Late-night shopping (until 8pm) is on Thu in the West End and Wed in Knightsbridge.

• Banks: Mon–Fri 9.30–5; a few remain open later or open on Sat mornings. *Bureaux de change* generally have longer opening hours. ATMs are abundant.

• Post offices: Usually Mon–Fri 9–5.30, Sat 9–12.30.

NEWSPAPERS AND MAGAZINES

Newspapers include the *Financial Times*, *The Daily Telegraph*, *The Independent*, *The Guardian*, *The Daily Mail* and *The Times*, Sunday papers include *The Sunday Times*, *Sunday Telegraph*, *The Observer* and *Independent on Sunday*. Free papers (Mon–Fri) are *Metro* and *London Evening Standard*, which is strong on entertainment and nightlife (www.thisislondon.co.uk). *Time Out* (www.timeout.com), published weekly on Wed), lists almost everything going and is free.

TIPPING

Many restaurants add a 12.5 percent service charge. For taxis, hairdressers and other services, 10 percent is acceptable. Tips are not usual in theaters, cinemas or concert halls, or in pubs or bars (unless there is table service).

EMBASSIES

Australian High Commission	✉ Australia House, Strand, WC2 ☎ 020 7379 4334, www.uk.embassy.gov.au
Canadian High Commission	✉ Canada House, Trafalgar Square, SW1 ☎ 020 7004 6000, www.unitedkingdom.gc.ca
New Zealand High Commission	✉ New Zealand House, 80 Haymarket, SW1 ☎ 020 7930 8422, www.nzembassy.com
Embassy of the US	✉ 24 Grosvenor Square, W1 ☎ 020 7499 9000, http://london.usembassy.gov

MAILING A LETTER

Stamps are sold at post offices and some newsagents and shops. Trafalgar Square Post Office stays open late: ✉ William IV Street, WC2 ⏰ Mon–Fri 8.30–6.30, Sat 9–5.30. Letter boxes are red.

TELEVISION

- The five most watched channels in Britain are BBC1, BBC2, ITV1, Channel 4 and Channel 5. The BBC is funded by a licence fee and there is no advertising on any BBC channels.
- Relatively few homes in Britain have cable, although it is increasing. Digital terrestrial and digital satellite television services can be received in all homes, with a large number of channels and wide variety of content, available either free or through subscription. Programs can also be viewed on the Internet and 3G mobile (cellphones).

STUDENTS

Holders of an International Student Identity Card (ISIC) will be able to obtain some good concessions on travel and entrance fees.

PUBLIC HOLIDAYS

- 1 Jan; Good Fri; Easter Mon; May Day (first Mon in May); last Mon in May; last Mon in Aug; 25 Dec; 26 Dec.
- Almost all attractions and shops close Christmas Day; many close 24 Dec, 1 Jan, Good Fri and Easter Sun as well. Some shops, restaurants and attractions remain open throughout, but check.

SENSIBLE PRECAUTIONS

- Keep valuables in a hotel or bank safe box.
- Note all passport, ticket and credit card numbers, and keep separately. Carry photocopies of the key pages of your passport.
- Make sure that bags are fully closed and keep them in sight at all times—do not put them on the floor or over the back of a chair.
- At night, try not to travel alone; if you must, either prebook a taxi (not a mini-cab) or keep to well-lit streets and use a bus or Tube train where there are other people.

PHONES

- London numbers (now 8 digits) are prefixed with the code 020 when dialling from outside the city. To call London from abroad, dial the country code 44, then just 20, then the 8-digit number.
- Public phones accept coins, phonecards and credit cards.
- For the operator tel 100. For the international operator or to reverse charges tel 155.
- Directory enquiries: There are many options; tel 0800 953 0720 for details and prices.
- To make international calls from the UK, dial 00, then the country code (1 for the US).
- Beware of high charges on numbers that start with 084, 087 or 09.
- Numbers starting 0800 are free.
- Before departure, consult with your cell/mobile phone provider on coverage and rates.

TOURIST INFORMATION

- **London Information Centre**
  Leicester Square, W1, tel 020 7437 4370, www.londontown.com, daily 10–6.

Books and Films

London's vitality, variety, glamor and squalor have always provided rich pickings for writers and film makers.

London: The Biography (2000), *Thames: Secret River* (2007) and *London Under* (2014) by historian Peter Ackroyd are essential background reading for visitors to the city. For fans of historical fiction, C.J. Sansom's Matthew Shardlake series (2003–11) evokes London at the time of Henry VIII.

Sixty famous authors pen portraits past and present in *City-Lit London* (2009) while in *An Alphabet of London* (2012) artist Christopher Brown chronicles the city in witty linocut illustrations. Muriel Spark used life in post-war Kensington as the setting for her novella *The Girls of Slender Means* (1963); in *A Severed Head* (1961), Iris Murdoch foresaw the sexual revolution and swinging London of the 1960s. The amusing *Bridget Jones's Diary* (1997) by Helen Fielding defined a generation of 30-something women living in London in the late 1990s.

With his autobiographical *Fever Pitch* (1992) and fictional *About a Boy* (1998), Nick Hornby took a different angle on youthful London, as did Hanif Kureishi in *The Buddha of Suburbia* (1990).

At the turn of the 21st century, multinational, multidenominational London was being explored by writers such as Zadie Smith in *White Teeth* (2001), Monica Ali in *Brick Lane* (2001) and Andrea Levy in *Small Island* (2004). *Spitalfields Life* began as a blog and the book (2012) is a gem.

Several of these novels have made their way onto the big screen, but for many people the most iconic movies are Michael Caine's lad-about-town *Alfie* (1966), the crime comedy *A Fish Called Wanda* (1988), the two *Bridget Jones* films (2001, 2004) and writer/director Richard Curtis's romantic comedies *Four Weddings and a Funeral* (1994), *Notting Hill* (1999) and *Love Actually* (2003), with the oh-so-English Hugh Grant playing the leading role in all three.

LONDON CLASSICS

Perhaps the most famous book about London is *The Diary of Samuel Pepys*, in which the observer, Pepys, recorded events from 1600 to 1669. Many of Charles Dickens' novels have London settings, including *Oliver Twist* (1837), *The Old Curiosity Shop* (1840), *Bleak House* (1853) and *Little Dorrit* (1857). In 1887, Sir Arthur Conan Doyle introduced his character Sherlock Holmes in the novel *A Study in Scarlet*. The legendary fictional detective lived at 221b Baker Street, W1. In William Thackeray's *Vanity Fair* (1847), Becky Sharp begins her adventures in Russell Square. Humorist P.G. Wodehouse, creator of the eccentric Jeeves and Wooster, based his Drones Club on several London gentlemen's clubs of the time (1920s).

Index

30 St. Mary Axe (The Gherkin) 66, 89

A

accommodations 9, 152–159
airports 164–165
Albert Memorial 66, 107
Apsley House (Wellington Museum) 9
architecture 4, 14, 18–19, 22–23, 48–51, 54–55
art 15, 19, 21, 32–35, 48–55, 123
auction houses 125

B

Bank of England Museum 49, 66
Banqueting House 14–15, 100, 104
bars and clubs 131–139
bed-and-breakfast 154
see also accommodations
Borough Market 8, 66–67, 82
British Library 17, 67
British Museum 9, 16–17, 98
Brompton Oratory 67
Buckingham Palace 4, 9, 18–19, 101, 104
buses 166

C

Canary Wharf 4, 76, 113
Changing the Guard 79
Charles Dickens Museum 67
Chelsea Physic Garden 76
children 9
Chinatown 95
Chiswick House 76
churches and cathedrals
Holy Trinity, Sloane Square 71
St. Bartholomew-the-Great 73
St. James's, Piccadilly 73, 101, 138
St. Paul's Cathedral 4, 9, 44–45, 57, 88, 92
Southwark Cathedral 57, 74, 82
Temple Church 74
Westminster Abbey 62–63, 100
Churchill War Rooms 67–68, 100, 105
cinemas 133–136
City Hall 68, 82
Clarence House 68, 101
Cleopatra's Needle 68
climate 162
Courtauld Gallery 51, 94
Covent Garden Piazza 69
Covent Garden to Regent's Park 69, 94–99
Cutty Sark 20

D

disabilities, visitors with 166
Docklands 4, 6, 77
Dulwich Picture Gallery 76

E

East End 6–7
eating out 39, 126, 142
see also restaurants
embassies 169
emergencies 168
entertainment 9, 128–139
Eros 69
etiquette 142, 147, 169
events and festivals 162
excursions
Hampton Court Palace 78
Windsor 79
see also tours

F

film *see* cinemas
Firepower Museum 76
Fleet Street to the Tower 88–93
Foundling Museum 69
Farther Afield 112–117

G

Garden Museum 69
The Gherkin (30 St. Mary Axe) 66, 89
Golden Hinde II 69–70, 83
Green Park 8, 70
Greenwich 8, 20–21, 57, 112–117
Guildhall Art Gallery 70, 88

H

Ham House 76
Hampstead Heath 77
Hampton Court Palace 78
Handel House Museum 9, 70
Hayward Gallery 70
history 10–11, 14–15, 22–23, 58–59
HMS *Belfast* 70–71, 82
Holy Trinity, Sloane Square 71
hotels and hostels 9, 154–159
houses (*see* palaces)
Houses of Parliament 22–23, 56, 100, 104
Hyde Park 6, 8, 71, 106–111

I

Imperial War Museum 24–25, 86

J

Jewish Museum 77

K

Kensington Gardens 8, 26, 107, 110
Kensington Palace 26–27, 107, 110
Kenwood House 8, 77
Kew Gardens 8, 77, 116
Knightsbridge 28–29, 110

L

Leadenhall Building 71
libraries 17, 67
London Eye 30–31, 56, 83, 86
London Transport Museum 71
London Underground 5, 166
London Wetland Centre 77
ZSL London Zoo 72–73

M

Madame Tussaud's 72
maps 84–85, 90–91, 96–97, 102–103, 108–109, 114–115
medical treatment 168–169
Millennium Footbridge 4, 55
money 168
museums and galleries
Apsley House (Wellington Museum) 66
Bank of England Museum 49, 66
British Museum 9, 16–17, 98
Charles Dickens Museum 67
Churchill War Rooms 67–68, 100
Courtauld Gallery 51, 94
Dulwich Picture Gallery 76
Firepower Museum 76
Foundling Museum 69
Guildhall Art Gallery 70, 88
Handel House Museum 9, 70
Hayward Gallery 70
Imperial War Museum 24–25, 71
Jewish Museum 77
London Transport Museum 71
Museum of London 32–33, 88, 92
Museum of London Docklands 77
National Gallery 34–35, 100, 104

National Maritime Museum 21, 112
National Portrait Gallery 36–37, 100, 104
Natural History Museum 38–39, 106, 110
Petrie Museum 72
Photographers' Gallery 72
Queen's Gallery 19
Royal Academy of Arts 73
Science Museum 46–47, 106, 110
Sir John Soane's Museum 9, 74, 94
Somerset House 50–51, 98
Tate Britain 52–53, 104
Tate Modern 4, 54–55, 57, 83, 86
Victoria and Albert Museum 60–61, 106, 110
V&A Museum of Childhood 77
Wallace Collection 75
Whitechapel Art Gallery 77
music venues 133–139

N
National Gallery 34–35, 100, 104
National Maritime Museum 21, 112
National Portrait Gallery 36–37, 100, 104
Natural History Museum 38–39, 106, 110
nightlife *see* entertainment

O
Old Royal Naval College 20, 112
Olympic Games 4, 11
opening hours 169

P
palaces and houses
Banqueting House 14–15, 100, 104
Buckingham Palace 4, 9, 18–19, 101, 104
Chiswick House 76
Clarence House 68, 101
Ham House 76
Kensington Palace 26–27, 107, 110
Kenwood House 77
St. James's Palace 101
Somerset House 50–51, 94, 98
Spencer House 9, 75
parks and gardens 6, 9, 20, 25, 42–46, 70–73, 76–77, 100, 104, 107, 110, 113, 116
Peter Pan statue 27, 72
Petrie Museum 72
Photographers' Gallery 72
population 4
Portobello Road Market 40–41, 116
public holidays 170

Q
Queen Elizabeth II 11, 18–19, 79

R
Regent's Park 8, 9, 72–73, 94
restaurants 8, 140–151
Royal Academy of Arts 73
Royal Family 10–11, 18–19, 24–25, 63, 68, 101, 106
Royal Observatory 21, 113

S
St. Bartholomew-the-Great 73
St. James's Palace 101
St. James's Park 6, 42–43, 100, 104
St. James's, Piccadilly 73, 101, 138
St. Katharine Docks 73, 89
St. Paul's Cathedral 4, 9, 44–45, 57, 88, 92
Science Museum 9, 46–47, 106, 110
SEA LIFE London Aquarium 74
Shakespeare's Globe 48–49, 83, 139
The Shard 74, 82
shopping 8, 26–27, 38–39, 67, 69, 118–127
Sir John Soane's Museum 9, 74, 94
Soho 95
Somerset House 50–51, 94, 98
South Bank 4, 28, 82–87
South Kensington 17
Southwark Cathedral 57, 74, 82
Spencer House 75

T
Tate Britain 52–53, 104
Tate Modern 4, 54–55, 57, 83, 86
taxis 166–167
temperatures 162
Temple Church 74
Temple of Mithras 75, 89
Thames river cruise 56–57, 101, 104
theatres 133–139
Timeline 10–11
tipping 147, 169
tourist information 163, 167, 170
tours
Around Hyde Park 106–111
Covent Garden to Regent's Park 94–99
Fleet Street to the Tower 88–93
Farther Afield 112–117
South Bank 82–87
Westminster and St. James's 100–105
see also excursions
Tower of London 4, 57, 58–59, 89, 92
Trafalgar Square 75, 100
transport 4–5, 7, 164–167
travel insurance 168
travel planning 162–170
The Tube 5, 166

V
Victoria and Albert Museum 60–61, 106, 110
V&A Museum of Childhood 77
visas 168

W
Wallace Collection 75
websites 163
Westminster Abbey 62–63, 100, 105
Westminster and St. James's 100–105
Whitechapel Art Gallery 77
Windsor 63, 79

Z
zoo 72–73

The Automobile Association would like to thank the following photographers, companies and picture libraries for their assistance in the preparation of this book.

Abbreviations for the picture credits are as follows – (t) top; (b) bottom; (c) center; (l) left; (r) right; (AA) AA World Travel Library.

2i AA/S. Montgomery; 2ii AA/N. Setchfield; 2iii AA/J. Tims; 2iv AA/S. Montgomery; 2v AA/J. Tims; 3i AA/J. Tims; 3ii AA/J. Tims; 3iii AA/R. Mort; 3iv AA/S. Montgomery; 4tl AA/S. Montgomery; 5 AA/J. Tims; 6c Brian Anthony/Alamy; 6/7t GeoPic/Alamy; 6/7tc Kathy deWitt/Alamy; 6/7b Stuart Forster/Alamy; 7c Bombaert Patrick/Alamy; 8/9i AA/S. Montgomery; 8/9ii AA/J. Tims; 8/9iii AA/J. Tims; 8/9iv AA/N. Setchfield; 8/9v AA/J. Tims; 8/9vi AA/N. Setchfield; 10bl AA/J. Tims; 10br The Art Archive/Alamy; 11bl Mary Evans Picture Library/Alamy; 11br AA/J. Tims; 12 AA/N. Setchfield; 14tl AA/J. Tims; 14tr AA/S. Montgomery; 14cr/15c AA/J. Tims; 15tl AA/J. Tims; 16t AA/J. Tims; 17tl AA/N. Setchfield; 17tr AA/J. Tims; 17c AA/J. Tims; 18t/19tl AA/J. Tims; 19tc AA/S. Montgomery; 19tr Courtesy Royal Collection 2011, Her Majesty Queen Elizabeth II/Derry Moore; 19c Monica Wells/TTL; 20t AA/N. Setchfield; 21tl AA/AA; 21cl AA/S and O Mathews; 21c AA/N. Setchfield; 22t/23tl AA/J. Tims; 22c/23cl AA/J. Tims; 23c AA/J. Tims; 23tr AA/J. Tims; 24/25 AA/J. Tims; 25tl AA/J. Tims; 25tr AA/J. Tims; 25c AA/J. Tims; 26 London Stills; 27tl AA/J. Tims; 27tr AA/S. Montgomery; 27cl London Stills; 27cr AA/J. Tims; 28 Courtesy Harvey Nichols; 29tl Courtesy Swarovski/Yellow Door; 29tr Travelshots.com/Alamy; 29cl Courtesy Harvey Nichols; 29cr AA/S. Montgomery; 30 Courtesy EDF Energy London Eye/British Tourist Authority/James McCormick; 31tl Courtesy EDF Energy London Eye; 31tr Courtesy EDF Energy London Eye; 31c Courtesy EDF Energy London Eye; 32/33tl Courtesy Museum of London; 33tr AA/J. Tims; 33cr AA/J. Tims; 34/35 Ronald Weir/TTL; 35tl AA/J. Tims; 35cl AA/J. Tims; 35c AA/J. Tims; 35tr Courtesy The National Gallery; 36 Courtesy The National Portrait Gallery; 37tl Courtesy The National Portrait Gallery/Andrew Putler; 37tr AA/J. Tims; 37cl AA/S. Montgomery; 37cr AA/J. Tims; 38l AA/N. Setchfield; 38tr/39tl AA/M. Jourdan; 38cr/39cl Courtesy Natural History Museum; 39tr Courtesy Natural History Museum/D. Adams; 40/41 Pawel Libera Images/Alamy; 41tr London Stills; 41cr AA/M. Jourdan; 42 David Noton/TTL; 43tl AA; 43tr SJ Images/Alamy 44l London Stills 44tr/45tl Courtesy St Paul's Cathedral/Peter Smith; 44br AA/AA; 45bl AA/AA; 45r AA/S. Montgomery; 46l Courtesy Science Museum; 46tr/47tl AA/J. Tims; 46br/47bl AA/J. Tims; 47r Courtesy Science Museum; 48l AA/R. Turpin; 48/49 AA/S. Montgomery; 50tl AA/J. Tims; 50tr/51tl The Courtauld Gallery/J. Tims; 50cr/51cl AA/J. Tims; 51tr The Courtauld Gallery/J. Tims; 52t AA/S. Montgomery; 53tl AA/S. Montgomery; 53cl AA/S. Montgomery; 53tr AA/S. Montgomery; 54tl AA/N. Setchfield; 54tr/55tl AA/J. Tims; 54cr AA/S. Montgomery; 55cl AA/S. Montgomery; 55tr Courtesy Herzog & de Meuron/Hayes Davidson; 56t/57tl AA/C. Sawyer; 56cl AA/T. Woodcock; 56cr/57cl AA/J. Tims; 57tr Courtesy London Duck Tours Ltd; 57cr AA/J. Tims; 58t AA/S. Montgomery; 59tl AA/S. Montgomery; 59tr AA/S. Montgomery; 59c AA/S. Montgomery; 60t/61tl Maurice Crooks/Alamy; 61tr Courtesy Victoria and Albert Museum/Alan Williams; 61cr Courtesy Victoria and Albert Museum/R. Waite; 62tl Tom Mackie/TTL; 62tr AA/J. Tims; 62cr/63cl AA/J. Tims; 63tl AA/J. Tims; 63tr AA/J. Tims; 64t AA/R. Mort; 66bl AA/J. Tims; 66br AA/S. Montgomery; 67bl AA/J. Tims; 67br AA/J. Tims; 68b AA/N. Setchfield; 69bl AA/J. Tims; 69br AA/J. Tims; 70b AA/S. McBride; 71b AA/N. Setchfield; 72bl AA/J. Tims; 72br AA/J. Tims; 73bl AA/S. Montgomery; 73br Courtesy Zoological Society of London; 74bl AA/S. Montgomery; 74br AA/J. Tims; 75b AA/J. Tims; 76bl AA/P. Kenward; 76br Courtesy Museum of London; 78bl AA/D. Forss; 78br AA/D. Forss; 79bl AA/W. Voysey; 79br AA/J. Tims; 80 AA/S. Montgomery; 82tr AA/J. Tims; 82cl AA/S. Montgomery; 82br AA/M. Jourdan; 83tr AA/S. Montgomery; 83cl AA/R. Turpin; 83br Courtesy EDF Energy London Eye; 86t NEW 2015 AA/J. Tims; 86c AA/J. Tims; 86b AA/S. Montgomery; 87 AA/J. Tims; 88tr AA/N. Setchfield; 89tr AA/S. Montgomery; 89 lower c AA/W. Voysey; 92tr Courtesy Museum of London; 92cr Courtesy St Paul's Cathedral/Peter Smith; 92br AA/S. Montgomery; 93b Courtesy Transport for London/Hayes Davidson; 94l N. Setchfield/Alamy; 94b The Courtauld Gallery/J. Tims; 95tr AA/J. Tims; 95br AA/J. Tims; 98tr AA/N. Setchfield; 98br The Courtauld Gallery/J. Tims; 100t Courtesy The National Portrait Gallery/Andrew Putler; 100cr AA/J. Tims; 101t London Stills; 101bl AA/C. Sawyer 104i AA/J. Tims; 104ii AA/S. Montgomery; 104iii AA/J. Tims; 104iv London Stills; 104v AA/S. Montgomery; 104vi AA/S. Montgomery; 104vii AA/S. Montgomery; 104viii AA/N. Setchfield; 105tr AA/B. Smith; 106l Courtesy Victoria and Albert Museum; 107tr AA/J. Tims; 107b AA/S. Montgomery; 110i AA/P. Kenward; 110ii AA/P. Kenward; 110iii AA/T. Woodcock; 110iv AA/J. Tims; 110v Courtesy Victoria and Albert Museum/Morley von Sternberg; 112t AA/S and O Mathews; 112br David Noton/TTL; 113t AA/S and O Mathews; 113cl AA/W. Voysey; 116tr AA/AA; 116cr AA/M. Jourdan 116br Courtesy Royal Botanic Gardens, Kew/A.McRobb; 118 AA/J. Tims; 120/121i AA/S. Montgomery; 120/121ii AA/P. Kenward; 120/121iii AA/R. Turpin; 120/121iv AA/R. Strange; 120/121v AA/M. Trelawny; 120/121vi AA/S. Montgomery; 125br AA/J. Tims; 127br AA/S. Montgomery; 128 AA/J. Tims; 130/131i AA/J. Tims; 130/131ii AA/J. Tims; 130/131iii AA/M. Jourdan; 130/131iv AA/S. Montgomery; 130/131v AA/J. Tims; 134 AA/J. Tims; 139 AA/R. Turpin; 140 AA/J. Tims; 142ri AA/AA; 142ii AA/M. Jourdan; 142iii AA/N. Setchfield 142iv AA/J. Tims; 146bl AA/N. Setchfield; 146br AA/J. Tims; 148 AA/N. Setchfield 152 AA/R. Mort; 154i AA/W. Voysey; 154ii AA/J. Tims; 154iii OneOff Travel/Alamy; 154iv VIEW Pictures Ltd/Alamy; 157 AA/S. Montgomery; 158 AA/J. Tims; 160 AA/S. Montgomery.

Every effort has been made to trace the copyright holders, and we apologize in advance for any unintentional omissions or errors. We would be pleased to apply any corrections in a following edition of this publication.

London 25 Best

WRITTEN BY Louise Nicholson
ADDITIONAL WRITING AND UPDATING BY Sue Dobson
SERIES EDITOR Clare Ashton
COVER DESIGN Chie Ushio, Yuko Inagaki
DESIGN WORK Tracey Butler
IMAGE RETOUCHING AND REPRO Jacqueline Street-Elkayam

© AA MEDIA LIMITED 2015 (registered office: Fanum House, Basing View, Basingstoke, Hampshire RG21 4EA, registered number 06112600).

All rights reserved. Published in the United States by Fodor's Travel, a division of Random House LLC, New York, a Penguin Random House Company, and in Canada by Random House of Canada Limited, Toronto. No maps, illustrations, or other portions of this book may be reproduced in any form without written permission from the publisher.

Fodor's is a registered trademark of Random House LLC.

Published in the United Kingdom by AA Publishing

ISBN 978-1-1018-7945-0

ELEVENTH EDITION

All details in this book are based on information supplied to us at press time. Always confirm information when it matters, especially if you're making a detour to visit a specific place. Fodor's expressly disclaims any liability, loss, or risk, personal or otherwise, that is incurred as a consequence of the use of any of the contents of this book.

SPECIAL SALES
This book is available for special discounts for bulk purchases for sales promotions or premiums. For more information, email specialmarkets@randomhouse.com.

Color separation by AA Digital Department
Printed and bound by Leo Paper Products, China

10 9 8 7 6 5 4 3 2 1

A05314
Mapping © Crown copyright and database rights 2015 Ordnance Survey. 100021153.

Titles in the Series

- Amsterdam
- Barcelona
- Boston
- Budapest
- Chicago
- Dubai
- Dublin
- Edinburgh
- Florence
- Hong Kong
- Istanbul
- Las Vegas
- Lisbon
- London
- Madrid
- Milan
- Montréal
- Munich
- New York City
- Orlando
- Paris
- Rome
- San Francisco
- Seattle
- Shanghai
- Singapore
- Sydney
- Tokyo
- Toronto
- Venice
- Washington, D.C.